Power To Get Wealth

by

Luther Blackwell

Power To Get Wealth

by

Luther Blackwell

VINCOM, INC.
Tulsa, Oklahoma

2nd Printing 1993

Power To Get Wealth
ISBN No. 0-927936-35-6.
Copyright © 1992 by
Luther Blackwell
P. O. Box 145
Cortland, OH 44410

Published by
VINCOM, Inc.
P. O. Box 702400
Tulsa, OK 74170

Contents

Foreword

**But thou shalt remember the Lord thy God: for it
is he that giveth thee power to get wealth....**
Deuteronomy 8:18a

Yes, child of God, we have been given the power to
get wealth. But why? Is it to buy a Corvette or a Lear Jet?
No! The rest of the verse tells the whole story.

**...That he may establish his covenant which he
sware unto thy fathers, as it is this day.**
Deuteronomy 8:18b

God has given to each believer the power to get wealth
so that His covenant can be established. The word *establish*
in this context means "founded and grounded financially"
so that no economic problem may hinder or prevent the
building of His Kingdom.

You cannot be a part of establishing His covenant if you
are still bound by the old teachings and traditions that have
made the Word of God of no effect in your life. For too long,
the Church has held a "poverty is holy" mentality which
has prevented the release of an abundant financial harvest
into the Body of Christ. Unfortunately, many Christians still
believe there is something wrong with a man who has a
lot of money. They possess the unscriptural attitude of,
"Oh, God, if I just had enough. Lord, just give me enough
to provide for my family."

Have you ever prayed like that? Sure, you have, but
don't ever pray like that again!

Child of God, it costs money to bring in God's harvest,
and the Church of our Lord and Savior will never have the
finances to do it as long as the saints have a "just enough"

vii

attitude. We can only bring in the end-time harvest when Christians learn how to have more than enough to supply the funds necessary to establish His covenant on the earth.

Jesus did not have a "just enough" mentality and neither should those who follow after Him. In his book, Pastor Blackwell gives very clear illustrations that Jesus did not operate in need or lack. His practical insights into this scriptural truth will be a particular blessing to the Body of Christ.

Lord God, right now I ask that You reveal Yourself to every precious saint who picks up this book. Let each person read this book without any further interference from the enemy. In the strong name of Jesus, I loose understanding and revelation knowledge to the Body of Christ that they may walk in abundance, knowing that they have the power to get wealth. Father, free every believer from the lure and bondage of debt that they might truly walk in financial freedom. I call it done. Amen.

John Avanzini

Acknowledgments

Special thanks to a few people without whom this book would be slightly less than possible.

Accolades of praise are befitting at this time to express to such persons my gratitude.

Thank you, Bill White, for taking the truths of this series, and in turn, using them in my behalf to bring me great wealth.

Thank you, Cassandra, Dianne, Valeria and Karen, for totally availing yourselves for this project.

Thank you, Richard Ablondi, for taking our concepts and putting them in picture form. Your gift to our lives has certainly generated within us continuous praise.

Thank you, Lisa Mack, for all of the punctuation marks, changes in sentence structure and technical labor that you gave. You are very meticulous, and in this way, you constantly serve.

Connie Manning is saluted for the tedious job of ''listening'' to every word I have spoken on this subject matter, in order that a viable transcript and outline could be ascertained from the tapes.

Special thanks to my church administrator, Cathy A. Chilton, who, in my opinion, is the epitome of dedication, commitment and loyalty. Her excellent spirit keeps us moving in a near flawless vain.

To Bishop Dwight H. McDaniels, Jr., my father-in-law, I thank you for the principles of finance that you have deeply instilled within me over the years. Most of all, I thank you for your personal gift to my life, my beautiful wife, Lois.

Lois, my wife, continues to be a stabilizing and unwavering force in my life. I am constantly strengthened by her love and encouragement. Our offspring are a continual blessing to our lives and ministry — Stacy, our eldest, Alana, Lucien, our beloved son, and Meaghan.

Introduction
Power and Wealth

Power and *wealth* — two strong emotive words which have constantly caused controversy in the Body of Christ. Yes, we all know that God supplies our needs. The controversy begins when we attempt to work out *if* and *how* we participate in that process. Do we *name it* and *claim it?* "Oh, God, I know You are my Father. I know You want to treat me. See that sable grey Cadillac? I believe it's for me. Deliver it to me, complete with sheepskin seat covers. Amen." Or, do we swing to the other extreme, where it seems simpler to praise God and leave the decisions and consequences of power and wealth in His hands? "God, You supply my needs. I don't *need* a car. I can walk to work. If you want me to have one, I know You will provide it for me. Lord, I trust You and leave the decision to You."

A fundamental question underlying if or how we participate in the process of getting wealth is, "What exactly is wealth from the Bible's standpoint? Does it really mean two Cadillacs and a ten-bedroom home, or a million dollars in the bank?"

One Hebrew word for wealth is *hon*. It is found in Psalms and Proverbs and simply translates *enough* or *sufficiency*. Thus, when the Bible talks about wealth, it is not talking about megabucks, property all over the world or vacations on the Riviera. It is not talking about becoming a future billionaire or aiming to be another Bill Cosby, pulling in $115 million a year. No, when the Bible talks about wealth, it is talking about having enough — enough food on the table, enough clothes for the children, enough money to put them through school, enough money to pay the utility bills at the end of the month, enough money so we don't have to penny pinch and struggle year after year.

Biblical wealth is having enough to bless God, bless your family and bless others.

As a pastor, I have often researched the relationship between power and wealth in order to share insights with my congregation. One of the discoveries I made while undertaking this study was that it is God's will for us to prosper, both in the spiritual and in the physical/material realms, and it is God who initiates prosperity.

We can see this clearly in the life of Abram. God called him out from his relatives and country. Abram was a heathen, a Chaldean, but God selected him. In reading Genesis 12, you will discover that the blessings that came to Abram were not something that he pursued. It was something that God, of His own choosing, initiated.

> **Now the Lord said to Abram, "Go forth from your country and your kindred and your father's house to the land that I will show you.**
>
> **"And I will make of you a great nation, will bless you, and make your name great, so that you will be a blessing.**
>
> **"I will bless those who bless you, and him who curses you I will curse; and by you all the families in the earth shall bless themselves."**
>
> **Genesis 12:1-3**

Notice, it is God recounting all He will do for Abram, not the other way around.

Again in Genesis 15:1, we are told:

> **After these things the word of the Lord came to Abram in a vision, "Fear not, Abram, I am your shield; *your reward shall be very great.*"**

God intended all along to bless Abram.

As we read on through the story in Genesis, we see that Abram continued to live in obedience to God.

> When Abram was ninety-nine years old the Lord appeared to Abram, and said to him, "I am God Almighty; walk before me, and be blameless.
>
> "And I will make my covenant between me and you, and will multiply you exceedingly."
>
> Genesis 17:1,2

In the Abrahamic covenant, as we call it, God promises to multiply Abram exceedingly. This was God's idea. He had a plan to bring it about in Abram's life.

In Genesis 13:1,2, we read:

> So Abram went up from Egypt, he and his wife, and all that he had, and Lot with him, into the Negeb.
>
> Now Abram was very rich in cattle, in silver, and in gold.

God was already fulfilling His original promise to Abram. He multiplied Abram's livestock, silver and gold, making him exceedingly wealthy.

God is in the business of prospering. Just as He declared He would prosper Abram, He did. If God had a problem with prosperity, then it seems odd that He chose to use it as a sign to all that Abram was His chosen vessel.

Even with this understanding, it still came as a complete surprise to me in 1990 when God spoke very clearly to my heart, "This is the decade I have set aside for you to make money." What could that mean? Pastors, especially black pastors, weren't supposed to be rich! How would I make the money? What would I do with it? And why would God want me to make money anyway? Money-making was not one of my spiritual ideals. I discussed the matter with my wife, Lois, and together we began to seek God as to what His word to me could mean. I also began to study the Bible for more understanding.

Now, two years later, I can tell you, God's Word is true. Soon after He gave me the mandate to make money, unusual things began to happen in my life. Extraordinary situations and circumstances occurred. My income has tripled, and I now own five rental homes. I have also given much more to God's work than ever before, and I have found a new level of obedience to God's voice.

I have shared widely the principles and insights God has given me. As I have done so, I have discovered that many Christians are guided in the area of power and wealth by certain suppositions, some of them founded in the Word of God, many of them not.

Out of a concern to see balance in this area has come an audio-tape series, and now this book, *Power To Get Wealth.* The title comes from Deuteronomy 8:18. It occurs in the context of God reminding the children of Israel of all the blessings He has bestowed upon them. He recounts how He fed them manna, prevented their clothing from wearing out, spouted water from the rocks and multiplied their herds, their silver and their gold. Following this, God says to them:

> **Beware lest you say in your heart, "My power and the might of my hand have gotten me this wealth."**

> **You shall remember the Lord your God, for it is he who gives you** *power to get wealth.* **. . .**
> **Deuteronomy 8:17,18**

My prayer for you as you read this book is that you will discover the power to get wealth. Read it with an open heart. God is a God of new beginnings. Allow Him to plant new ideas and fresh insights into your mind.

> **Behold, I am doing a new thing; now it springs forth, do you not perceive it? I will make a way in the wilderness, and rivers in the desert.**
> **Isaiah 43:19**

1
A Clear Mind

Frank and his wife, Carol, felt God had called Frank to full-time service, so Frank quit his job. He and Carol and their small daughter lived *on faith*. Eventually, they ran short of money and had to sell their house. They continued living on about $400 a month, well below poverty level. Sometimes they lived with other families, at other times they lived in dormitory-type situations. Given time and two more children, the financial stress became almost unbearable.

Frank and Carol stopped talking about money. It was too painful a subject and often led to arguments. They sought help from their pastor who prayed with them. He also admonished them to have more *faith* and believe God for the money they so desperately needed. Still, none came.

Frank's co-workers encouraged him not to grow weary of well-doing. At the same time, their Christian friends involved in the *secular* world looked up to them as spiritual giants. "We think you are amazing. We could never live like this," they would say.

The financial pressure Frank and Carol felt continued to grow. They began to question how a God who loved them could leave them without money for the rent or new clothes for the baby. How would they ever put their children through college, or raise them to have a healthy view of "Jehovah Jireh," our provider? He seemed to be doing little to provide for their needs.

Finally, they reached the point where they were so confused and depressed that they needed some answers

1

— answers that worked. Carol ordered a copy of my tape series, "Power to Get Wealth." Gradually, they began to unravel themselves from their financial problems. Frank began to see that he had many false assumptions about God's role in finances. He began replacing the false assumptions with truth and slowly came to a place of understanding and balance regarding finances.

Frank is still in full-time ministry today. Through prayerful planning, he and Carol have been able to find a way out of the depressing financial pit they had fallen into. "Before any of this could happen," says Frank, "I had to recognize all the spiritual baggage I was carrying around. Once I was free from all that, I was able to see the real truth of God's Word regarding money. It became clear which direction we needed to go. Now, for the first time in eight years, I feel like I'm really in God's will *and* satisfied with my financial progress."

The Baggage We Carry

Like Frank, all of us carry around a certain amount of spiritual baggage regarding money. Some of us believe it is more godly and spiritual to own nothing. We equate poverty with Christlikeness. Whether consciously or unconsciously, we think that the poorer we are, the more God loves us and the holier we are.

Indeed, this view of spirituality and money seems to be the prevailing attitude of society. Watch the media reports or movies that portray virtuous or spiritual people. All too often they are typecast in the context of poverty or lack. On the other hand, rich Christians, be they televangelists or businessmen, are usually viewed with some suspicion by the media, as though some character weakness or aberration has led to their wealth.

Many of the Christians who have amassed wealth, or who own many material possessions, suffer the agony of constant guilt because of what they have. Deep down inside, they have a nagging doubt that perhaps they really aren't spiritual enough, because they haven't given it all up.

One of Satan's most common strategies is to keep us ignorant of the truth by distorting and twisting it. Thus, the first piece of spiritual armor Paul mentions in his letter to the Ephesians is the *girdle of truth*. Jesus said, **You will know the *truth*, and the *truth* will make you free** (John 8:32). Are you willing to examine the assumptions about faith and finances that you have collected over the years? Are you ready to hold them up to the truth of God's Word? It may require you to realign your thinking, as Frank had to do, but it will be well worth the effort, because you will be set free!

Distorted Assumptions

As I have taught and counselled with people on the topic of finance, I have discovered certain similar assumptions about Christianity and money. Below, I will discuss the ten most common of these assumptions.

Prayerfully consider them. Discuss them with your spouse, and do further Bible study on your own. What is important is that you know not only what you believe in regard to faith and finances, but *why* you believe what you believe.

1. *"I Must Be Poor Like Jesus"*

"I have decided to follow Jesus, no turning back, no turning back. The world behind me, the cross before me, no turning back, no turning back." Subconsciously, for many of us, the ideal of following Jesus involves following Him into a life of relative poverty.

How would we imagine Jesus to live if He were here today? Many of the people I talk to seem to think that if Jesus were alive today, He would live like a bag-man, pushing around all His worldly possessions in a discarded K-Mart trolley. He would sleep with the homeless and beg for a cup of coffee on the street. But such an understanding is far from the New Testament picture we have of Jesus.

When Jesus came to earth, He was born in a manger, the lowest of the low, born among the animals. We know the story backwards, but do we really stop to think about it? Why was He born in the manger? Because His parents arrived too late to rent a room in a hotel. Obviously, they had expected to stay in a hotel. Having a baby in a barn was probably as strange to them as it would be to us. Why were Joseph and Mary going to Bethlehem in the first place? Because they had to pay taxes, from which we can deduce that they must have had an income from which to pay the taxes.

Think about the "baby gifts" Jesus received: gold, frankincense and myrrh. These were expensive gifts. Mary wrapped Jesus in swaddling clothes, which were normally reserved for the children of royal lineage. God honored Jesus with material wealth at His birth.

Mary rode to Bethlehem on a donkey, and it is also interesting to note that Jesus rode a donkey into Jerusalem on Palm Sunday. In New Testament times, the donkey was the wealthy person's form of transportation. Poor men walked. Rich men rode.

At the time of Jesus' death, God had honored Him with many quality possessions. The soldiers divided His possessions and threw dice to decide who would get His robe. His robe was an expensive seamless robe, too good to tear and divide.

During His life, there is only one instance where Jesus refers to not having something material. It was when He said, **Foxes have holes, and birds of the air have nests; but the Son of man has nowhere to lay his head** (Matthew 8:20). And even this holds great spiritual significance.

Many times, exactly what Jesus needed was at His disposal. When He needed a boat, He knew where to get one. When He needed to pay His taxes, He sent Peter to find coins in a fish's mouth. When He needed transportation, it was waiting for Him. These situations, which appear to be the normal course of events for Jesus, do not show any sign that He lacked, wanted, needed, or struggled for things in the material realm.

I do not believe Jesus would be considered poor if He were here today, because He had all things available to Him. He lacked nothing He needed.

The misconceptions about Jesus and poverty arise when we confuse the physical and the spiritual realities to which He referred. In comparison to the position and relationship Jesus had with the Father in the heavenly realm prior to His becoming a man, He was immeasurably poor on earth. Yet, He willingly gave it up, divesting Himself of His former glory to become like a man. This is what happened in the spiritual realm. In no way does this imply that the same is true in the material realm, and that we, in turn, must become materially poor like Jesus — He wasn't!

2. *"Jesus will love me more if I'm poor"*

We often quote the words of Jesus, **You always have the poor with you** (Matthew 26:11), as an affirmation of the special affection Jesus had for the poor. But notice the words, *with you*. It does not say that you or I need to become one of them. Rather, Jesus is saying we are not to have an attitude or disposition that is unhealthy toward the poor, because they are in a state of want and lack. He is telling us to get used to the poor because they are always part of any social organization.

How true His words are. Every political system that has tried to eliminate the poor has failed. We have stark witness to this in the recent events in the Soviet Union and the fall of Communism. There is a natural sifting of people and wealth that occurs in any group over time. Jesus was merely stating a truism, not laying out the disposition we must assume if we are to be His followers.

3. *Spiritual Blessings Replace Physical Blessings*

I have had people tell me the spiritual blessings of the New Testament replace the physical blessings of the Old Testament. They often quote Ephesians 1:3:

Blessed be the God and Father of our Lord Jesus Christ, who has blessed us in Christ with every spiritual blessing in the heavenly places.

They say, "In the Old Testament, God gave people gold and silver, but in the New Testament, He replaced gold and silver with spiritual blessings." Often, the two are held to be mutually exclusive. You are either materially or spiritually blessed, but not both.

How can this be? After all, it was Jesus who said:

Think not that I have come to abolish the law and the prophets; I have come not to abolish them but to fulfil them.

For truly, I say to you, till heaven and earth pass away, not an iota, not a dot, will pass from the law until all is accomplished.

Matthew 5:17,18

If we sever the Old Testament from the New, we are making a grave mistake.

Did people in the Old Testament lead such materialistic lives that they could only gauge how much they were pleasing God by the material things they had accumulated? What about David? God taught him many deep truths about himself in the midst of both lack and plenty.

When it comes to material things, many Christians today tend to under-spiritualize the Old Testament and over-spiritualize the New Testament. There are plenty of examples where God spiritually blessed Old Testament characters and physically blessed New Testament ones.

We need only to think of Jesus' first recorded miracle — turning water into wine. Now, that doesn't sound very spiritual. Why did He do it? It seems He performed the miracle at His mother's request to avoid the host's embarrassment at not having bought enough wine to last the evening.

The truth is, Jesus was interested in peoples' material well-being just as He was interested in their spiritual well-being. This understanding strikes a blow at the very root that would try to divide the types of blessings God dispensed in the Old and New Testaments.

4. *Accumulation Equated to Evil Desires*

To some, wanting to accumulate money or material possessions is equated with evil desire. First Timothy 6:10 is their rallying cry:

> **For the love of money is the root of all evils; it is through this craving that some have wandered away from the faith and pierced their hearts with many pangs.**

They forget that it is the *love of money* which is the root of all evils, not money itself. It is true that at the bottom of evil is money or greed in its wider sense. The motive that drives people to kill, murder, steal, or prostitute themselves is most often money.

Handling money is not like handling dynamite. Money is a neutral thing, not something of which to be scared or from which to be backed away. If it were really something God abhorred, then surely He would not have left specific instructions on how it is to be used by godly men. It is only when we become so attached to money that God can't pry our affection from it that money becomes a *root of evil*.

Jesus felt very comfortable talking about money. Out of the forty parables which are recorded, twelve use money as a central theme. Think of the Lost Coin parable, the Talents, the Treasure Hidden in a Field, the Pearl of Great Price and the Two Debtors. We often think more ''warmly'' about the parables involving planting and harvesting. We like to imagine Jesus being close to the land, in touch with the working man's world, yet only seven of Jesus' parables are about planting and harvesting. Jesus was just as adept in talking about money as He was in talking about gardening or any other topic.

The greatest commandment Jesus tells us is, **Love the Lord your God with all your heart, and with all your soul, and with all your mind, and with all your strength** (Mark 12:30). Everything else in our lives, including money, must pale in relation to this commandment. If we fail to place money in its proper order, then it can easily become a root of evil in our lives. If, however, we bring it into line with God's priorities for our lives, then money and material things will become a great help and benefit to us rather than a hindrance. In fact, the Bible tells us, **Bread is made for laughter, and wine gladdens life, and money answers everything** (Ecclesiastes 10:19).

Much of what is accomplished for the Kingdom of God is made possible through money.

I do a weekly radio show in Cleveland, Ohio. Is the Cleveland radio station really interested in my message? Not particularly. Are they interested in my money? Definitely! When you want to get on the radio and preach the Gospel of Jesus Christ, you will need lots of money. If you're going to build a church building, it requires money. If you are going to distribute literature at a public function, it requires money. Even to run an outreach youth rally, it requires money. Everything you do requires money. It is true in your own household, and it is true in the household of the church as well.

We need to stop down-grading money as something carnal. It is a necessary avenue to the abundance in Kingdom living and ministry to which every believer has been called.

5. *God Will Take Care*

"I don't need to worry or think about money at all. God will take care of it for me." I don't know how many times people have told me this. Like the "root of evil" folk we mentioned previously, they also have their proof text from scripture.

> **Therefore I tell you, do not be anxious about your life, what you shall eat or what you shall drink, nor about your body, what you shall put on. Is not life more than food, and the body more than clothing?**
>
> **Look at the birds of the air: they neither sow nor reap nor gather into barns, and yet your heavenly Father feeds them. Are you not of more value than they?**
>
> **And which of you by being anxious can add one cubit to his span of life?**
>
> **And why are you anxious about clothing? Consider the lilies of the field, how they grow; they neither toil nor spin;**
>
> **Yet I tell you, even Solomon in all his glory was not arrayed like one of these.**
>
> Matthew 6:25-29

This passage tells us not to worry or be anxious about material things. The key word is *anxious*. There is a world of difference between anxiously worrying about something and taking care of it. For example, I care about my health. I watch what I eat and try to get a reasonable amount of exercise. If something unusual is happening to my body, I go to the doctor for a checkup. However, I am not anxious or worried about my health. I don't go to sleep fretting that my body may give out while I sleep and I will never wake up again. I do the best I can to keep my body in good health and leave the rest to God. I care, but I do not worry. There is a difference.

Never worry about material things. As Jesus pointed out, worry won't add another day to our lives, and our bodies are more important than what we clothe them in. Jesus put it another way in Luke 12:15: **Take heed, and beware of all covetousness; for a man's life does not consist in the abundance of his possessions.**

We are far more important than our external possessions. But as Jesus also points out in the passage from

Matthew 6, "I know you need these things, and if you get your priorities straight, I'll give them to you without a second thought" (my paraphrase).

6. *Getting Rich Disqualifies Me From Heaven*

And Jesus said to his disciples, "Truly, I say to you, it will be hard for a rich man to enter the kingdom of heaven."

Matthew 19:23

The context of this verse is Jesus' response to the rich young ruler who said he wanted to follow Jesus, but he was unprepared to leave his position and money behind. From this comes the false notion that we can't be rich and be saved at the same time. We misunderstand the principle Jesus is trying to convey and believe that if we get rich, we will automatically be disqualified from entering heaven.

I believe Jesus was saying to the rich young ruler that unless he was prepared to leave his money and his identity behind, he could not enter the Kingdom of God in the following sense: **For the kingdom of God is not food and drink but righteousness and peace and joy in the Holy Spirit** (Romans 14:17).

The kingdom of heaven is not an earthly kingdom. When we enter it, we leave our money, titles, influence and position at the gate. That is not to say we cannot have them here on earth, but that they are not a part of the kingdom of heaven. I am not rich in the kingdom of heaven, or poor, or black, or white, or old, or young, or slave, or free man. We are all one in Jesus Christ. If we cannot enter the kingdom of heaven as little children, uncaring of our earthly rank and privilege, we cannot enter at all. If this is what Jesus was referring to, then indeed there are no rich men in the kingdom of heaven.

7. *Man Does Not Live By Bread Alone*

In Luke 4:4, Jesus tells us, **Man shall not live by bread alone.** Thus, we infer that money is not to play a major role in our lives. Interestingly though, when Jesus says this,

He is quoting from Deuteronomy 8:3, the same chapter in which God declares to the Israelites that He has given them the power to make wealth (Deuteronomy 8:18). Let's look at Jesus' quote in the context of the verse in Deuteronomy.

And he humbled you and let you hunger and fed you with manna, which you did not know, nor did your fathers know; that he might make you know that man does not live by bread alone, but that man lives by everything that proceeds out of the mouth of the Lord.

God is saying, "Don't allow bread to become your focus. Ultimately, it comes from Me, so make Me your focus, and the bread will be there when you need it."

Jesus gives us a similar example in John 4. The disciples arrived from a food-buying expedition and began to encourage Jesus to eat something. **I have food to eat of which you do not know** was Jesus' reply in John 4:32. The disciples began questioning among themselves as to who brought Jesus food. They didn't grasp that Jesus was pointing out to them that man does not live by bread alone.

I believe there are times when you can be drawn so close to God that His Word dissipates your fleshly appetite and you do not hunger. Indeed, I can remember once sitting at my desk for sixteen hours without moving, nothing before me but the Bible. For sixteen hours, I was engulfed in the presence of the Lord, His Word satisfying my every need.

God can and will meet our needs, both material and physical, when we put our focus on Him. But this in no way implies that we are not to have money or material possessions. Remember, Deuteronomy 8:18 reveals that one of God's provisions for us is that He has given us the power to get wealth.

8. *My Reward Is In Heaven*

According to Luke 18:29,30, why should I worry about material possessions and money? After all, my reward is in heaven.

The difficulty with false assumptions is they are often half true! Think about what this scripture is saying:

> **Truly, I say to you, there is no man who has left house or wife or brothers or parents or children, for the sake of the kingdom of God,**
>
> **Who will not receive manifold more *in this time*, and in the age to come eternal life.**

It is true that we will receive our reward in the life to come, which is eternal life. But God also said we would receive *manifold more in this time.*

In the process of discipleship, God often requires that we give up certain things. We are confident of what we will receive as a result of our commitment and sacrifice in heaven, but did Jesus really mean it when He said we would receive manifold more *in this life?* Why not? It's there in black and white, just as clearly as is the reward we will receive in heaven.

9. *God Wants Me To Be Content With My Circumstances*

> **I have learned, in whatever state I am, to be content.**
>
> **I know how to be abased, and I know how to abound; in any and all circumstances I have learned the secret of facing plenty and hunger, abundance and want.**
>
> **I can do all things in him who strengthens me.**
> **Philippians 4:11-13**

What a challenge Paul's words are to us. He was a man who had faced great extremes in his life, yet he had found the secret of not becoming embittered or losing faith — contentment.

Being content does not mean we become lazy or disinterested. At the same time that Paul was content, he was also doing everything he could to get out of difficult situations. For example, consider his exile to Rome. It was Paul who pointed out to the centurion that he was a Roman citizen. It was Paul who insisted that Festus send him to Rome to be tried before Caesar. Paul had a keen mind, and he used it to try to find a way through the problems he faced.

Being content is not synonymous with being weak or allowing circumstances to totally dictate our direction in life. We are exhorted to change the things that are within our power to change, and to lean on God's grace to accept the rest. All too often, as Christians, we erroneously think we have to accept our situations exactly as they are and do nothing to change them. But Paul shows us that this is wrong. Contentment does not equate with inactivity and acceptance.

When it comes to the financial realm, by all means, be content. Don't strive and be eaten up by a desire for more. At the same time, look for ways out of the situation in which you find yourself. Paul did.

10. *Finances Cancel Faith*

I believe it is a trap to link faith and finances too closely. This can take two forms. On the one extreme we think, ''If I have enough faith, I won't need money anymore, because God alone will supply my needs.'' At the other extreme we say, ''If I have enough faith, I will always have an abundance of finances. Those finances are the tangible indication of my level of faith and God's pleasure toward me.''

I pondered these two ends of the spectrum for quite some time, trying to work out which ''faith camp'' had the weight of scripture on its side. But in the New Testament, money is simply not dealt with in these terms. Jesus talks in terms of little faith and great faith. In all of the Gospels, Jesus commended only two people for their great faith. One was a Canaanite woman who came to Him and asked Him to heal her demon-possessed daughter. Jesus said to her, **O woman, great is your faith! Be it done for you as you desire** (Matthew 15:28). The other person was the Centurion who asked Jesus to speak the word and his servant would be healed. Jesus said to him, **I tell you, not even in Israel have I found such faith** (Luke 7:9).

These two examples of "great faith" have a common thread. The faith that was exercised was on behalf of another person, and it did not involve material provision. Jesus never commended great faith in the realm of believing for material things.

Sometimes in the Bible, faith and finances are linked. At other times, they are not. If finances were always a result of faith, then Christians would all be rich, and non-Christians would all be poor. But we all know that isn't true. There are very rich ungodly people in the world and some very poor righteous people. To always link faith and finances is to over-simplify things.

The fallacy of using finances as a gauge of a person's faith has been around for a long time. In 1 Timothy 6:4,5 Paul writes:

> **He is puffed up with conceit, he knows nothing; he has a morbid craving for controversy and for disputes about words, which produce envy, dissension, slander, base suspicions,**

> **And wrangling among men who are depraved in mind and bereft of the truth, imagining that godliness is a means of gain.**

Paul is saying that there are those who see the Gospel as a "get-rich-quick scheme," a means of gain. Paul says people who think like this have depraved minds. Faith in Jesus Christ is not to be viewed in terms of monetary gain.

There is another major problem with the so-called "faith message." For some people, it tends to make faith work only in the material realm. The more you have, the more faith you have. If you don't have what the Jones' have, you don't have as much faith as they do. People who get caught up in this type of thinking end up assessing each other's houses and cars to determine the level of their faith. Driving an expensive car does not mean you have great faith. It may mean that you have great debt. Perhaps you have ten years of payments to make on it before it is completely yours.

Fifteen years ago I drove a Hornet. (If you don't know what that is, believe me, you don't want to know!) Ten years ago, I drove a Pontiac. Today I drive a Lincoln, a Volvo and a Mercedes-Benz. My faith in God has not gone up or down simply because of the type of car I own.

I didn't have Hornet-size faith fifteen years ago and Lincoln- or Mercedes-Benz-size faith today. This is not a matter to be analyzed in terms of faith. In many ways, the Pontiac was better than the Lincoln, because it was paid for! The Bible tells us there is only one way to gauge a person's faith, and it is very simple: . . . **Faith apart from works is dead** (James 2:26). It has nothing to do with material possessions. I believe I was doing good works fifteen years ago, and I trust that I am still doing good works today. If you want to judge levels of faith, then gauging good works is the only Biblical criteria to use.

Laying False Assumptions To Rest

These are the ten most common false assumptions which I believe keep Christians in financial bondage. I would encourage you to go back over these assumptions, and settle them once and for all in your heart and mind. You may want to search the scriptures until you are satisfied with your conclusions. Remember Jesus' parable about the folly of building a house on the sand? Unless you deal with these foundational issues, you will not have the firm foundation you need upon which to proceed and build your wealth. If you are going to chart a clear course through this process of accumulating wealth in a godly way, you need to know what you believe in regard to the power to get wealth and why.

2
Down to Basics

Many Christians think that by not having money, or by not adequately planning for the wise use of it when they do have it, they are leaving God in "control" in their finances. Many people who think this way are convinced they have a healthier outlook on "mammon" than the rest of the world does.

I have been a pastor for 25 years, and from my experience, this simply is not true. I have counselled with literally thousands of people over the years, and some of the most reoccurring problems I have had to deal with are related to money. One person is worried because he recently lost his job and his savings lasted only two weeks; another person's car is being repossessed; still another has been forced to take early retirement and has no money set aside for it. Some people are struggling in their marriages because, over the years, the tension of not having enough money has slowly and relentlessly worn away at the foundations of their relationships.

The people who seem the least trapped or caught up with money problems are not those who have no money. Quite the contrary. Those who are the most relaxed about money are the ones who have enough. Their minds are freed from the continual grind of worrying about how their kids will get through college, how they will ever replace their aging car, or where the money for next week's groceries will come from. Those who have enough money are free to enjoy what they have and get on with the other aspects of their lives.

Doing Our Part

The question ultimately arises in any discussion on finances as to our role in the accumulation of wealth. What is it, and what is God's role?

I believe it is a Biblical principle that we are to do the possible and leave God to do the impossible. So if we diligently do what we can with our financial situation, or any other aspect of our lives, then God will undertake to do the rest for us.

"God helps those who help themselves," the saying goes, and there is much truth in it. If we review the way God provides for people, we find that He seldom creates something from nothing or produces something that did not require the active participation of the recipients. Most often, He uses what the person has and either multiplies or utilizes it.

Consider for a moment the story of feeding the five thousand in John 6. Jesus asked the disciples to find out what resources were available from within the group. A small boy had five barley loaves and two fish. Jesus took this available resource, blessed it and multiplied it. Jesus could have just as easily by-passed that step and called a complete meal down from heaven. But He chose to take something already in existence and multiply it.

Again, the story in 2 Kings 4:1-7 reveals God employing a similar approach. A widow came running out to meet Elisha, beside herself with grief, because her two sons were about to be taken away by a creditor as slaves. Elisha's response to this situation is interesting. **What shall I do for you? Tell me; what have you in the house?** (2 Kings 4:2).

The widow told him that all that was left in the house was a jar of oil. So Elisha instructed her to go and borrow as many containers as she could. When she had done this, she was to shut the door and begin pouring from her bottle of oil into the containers. She did so and, miraculously, the containers kept being filled, until finally, when all the containers were full, the flow of oil ceased. God did not go beyond the woman's level of faith or effort.

To most people, manna is the epitome of supernatural provision. Yet, even the manna which God used to feed the Israelites as they fled from Egypt, came at the cost of personal effort. It required the cooperation of the people. I'm sure God could have easily guided the manna into neat little baskets outside each family's tent. But He chose not to. Instead, He blessed the children of Israel with as much food as they cared to bend down and pick up. At the end of each day, except the day before the Sabbath, the manna rotted so that each day they would have to go and gather fresh manna. There were no shortcuts. There was no picking up enough manna for a month and then relaxing to enjoy it. Every day they had to go out, sore backs, aching feet and all, and pick up what God had provided for them. I wonder if any of them said, "Hey, this can't be from God. He only gives us *good* gifts, not gifts for which we have to work. Let's wait on Him some more until He really provides for us."

Such a statement may seem ridiculous given the abundance of the manna. Unfortunately, many of us today exhibit such thinking. We see a way we could be provided for, but we dismiss it as "worldly" because it involves a little planning, a little work, a little effort on our part. So we reject this means of provision in favor of waiting for God to miraculously zap something into our hands. This won't happen. Manna was miraculous provision, but it was down on the ground, not piled up neatly outside the tents. If you wanted this provision, you had to bend and lift. Effort! We need to get the idea of effort fixed firmly in our hearts and minds in relationship to provision.

God, Creator of this amazing universe we inhabit, has planned ways for us to cooperate with Him in building our wealth. He will do His part as long as we do ours. He gives us *power* to get wealth. This requires that we do something and is vastly different from God simply giving us wealth.

The Four Powers

> I passed by the field of a sluggard, by the vineyard of a man without sense;
>
> And, lo, it was overgrown with thorns; the ground was covered with nettles, and its stone wall was broken down.
>
> Then I saw and considered it; I looked and received instruction.
>
> A little sleep, a little slumber, a little folding of the hands to rest,
>
> And poverty will come upon you like a robber, and want like an armed man.
>
> Proverbs 24:30-34

In this passage, we see what I have termed the "four powers" of wealth-building. We need each of these four powers functioning in a balanced way in our lives if we are to build and maintain wealth. Let's look at each of them briefly.

Notice that the man mentioned had a label. He was called a *sluggard*. So we're dealing with the field of a sluggard. *Sluggard* is not a kind word. It means someone who is lazy, lethargic and has a bad reputation and name.

A *good name* is the first of the four powers of wealth-building. A good name is particularly important in today's technological world where a good portion of our financial track record is carried on our credit record that is available for a large number of people to peruse. Without a good name, a person will be severely handicapped in his attempt to build wealth.

> A good name is to be chosen rather than great riches, and favor is better than silver or gold.
>
> Proverbs 22:1

Perhaps you have already blown your good name. Your bad credit record haunts your efforts to gain ascendancy over your financial situation. Later in this book, you will discover ways to redeem a bad credit record, ways that will enable you to clear your name and start over again. Your credit record can become a source of blessing to you rather than the curse it has been.

The second power upon which wealth is built is *knowledge*. The sluggard seemed to be without sense or knowledge. He had no idea what was about to happen to him. He did not know the perils of a broken fence, that predators would come in and eat his produce, nor did he realize how difficult it is to pick produce among nettles.

Knowledge is a highly-prized commodity in the Bible, and it is a highly-prized commodity in building wealth today. Without it, we can have all the good intentions in the world and still not advance. God is a God of knowledge, and we are created in His image. He expects us to gain the knowledge we need and then use it. Ignorance is no excuse for inactivity in the Christian life.

> **Keep hold of instruction, do not let go; guard her, for she is your life.**
>
> **Proverbs 4:13**

The third power is *discipline*. A few "lucky" people manage to achieve wealth without discipline, but no one *maintains* wealth without it. Again, Proverbs gives us insight:

> **When your eyes light upon it** (money), **it is gone; for suddenly it takes to itself wings, flying like an eagle toward heaven.**
>
> **Proverbs 23:5**

It may seem incredible, but 60 percent of the people who win the lottery are broke within five years. They had the opportunity of a lifetime, but their money had wings.

> **A little sleep, a little slumber, a little folding of the hands....**
>
> **Proverbs 24:33**

If we are going to prosper and build wealth, then we need to stop sitting around dreaming about how it will be when we win the lottery, or when a rich aunt dies and leaves us an inheritance. We must get our finances in order *now* — today!

Christians are some of the laziest people I know. Sometimes church even encourages us to be that way. If we see a car that we really like, most often we are not encouraged to save for it, or to work hard to earn the money to pay for it. Instead, we take the easy route. We go to a prayer meeting and ask God to touch Wendell or Vanessa's heart so they will buy the car for us. Or we ask a brother in the church to make us an interest-free loan to buy the car (usually with an eye to having the debt forgiven at some later date).

But God never seems to honor those who sit waiting for a handout. If you have a handout mentality, then it's time to get free of it. Leave your excuses behind: "You don't understand my plight, my dilemma, my need, my color, my parentage." Such excuses will only paralyze you. If you don't leave them behind, I can guarantee that in a few short years, you will be in the same, or even a worse, financial situation. God understands your situation completely, but He will not move a finger to do anything about it while you continue to wallow in self-pity, instead of actively pursuing a way through your problems.

God-Given Opportunities

The first three pillars of building wealth are dependent upon our effort. It is within our power to develop and maintain a good name, to acquire knowledge and to discipline ourselves in the area of finances. You may be wondering where God fits into all of this. Does He have a role and responsibility in wealth-building? Yes, He does, and it is quite simple. It is God's part to provide, or guide, us into the opportunities which will facilitate wealth-building. That is the fourth power — God-given *opportunities.*

When we look back at the sluggard in Proverbs, the one thing he had going for him was the opportunity to make it. The writer **passed by the *field* of a sluggard, by the *vineyard* of a man without sense** (Proverbs 24:30). This tells us that the sluggard had the opportunity to be financially stable. God had blessed him with property, but he did not use the opportunity wisely.

As I have shared this message over the years, I have seen God do amazing things. When people finally understand the Biblical view of wealth and their part in God's plan, He releases great opportunities to them for making money.

Once you bring discipline into your life, you actively seek to gain knowledge and maintain your good name in all that you do. Then God will create for you the opportunities to make enough money to meet your needs and the needs of your family.

In the following chapters, we will look at the practical application of each of these four powers. They are like the four legs of a chair. If one leg is longer or shorter than the others, the chair will topple.

As you continue reading this book, consider *all* of the aspects that are presented. It is human nature to get better at the things we are already good at and to ignore those things in which we are weak. You may already be fairly knowledgeable in financial matters, but you need to boost your level of discipline or work on developing a good name. Don't continue to gain knowledge at the expense of the other powers. In order to build, maintain and enjoy wealth, each of the four powers must be in balance; otherwise, your wealth will slip away from you.

3

Knowledge

Adam sat staring blankly at me. Spread out on the desk between us were all of his financial records: folders, papers, lists and receipts. We had just spent two hours reviewing them together. "There's no way out, is there?" he flatly asked. As much as I hated to acknowledge it, I shook my head. "This is going to be a long, hard battle," I told him.

"If only I'd known, I'd never have gotten myself into this mess," he chastised himself.

My heart went out to Adam. His plan of provision seemed like such a good idea in the beginning. After he became a Christian, he looked for a way to support himself, and he started his own business. He had the expertise to do it, and it seemed so easy. He wasn't familiar with the tax laws relating to self-employment, so he had asked a few of his friends and got a general idea of how the tax laws worked. Or so he thought.

A year later, he showed up at my door, a very distressed young man. He was in over his head. He owed more than he could possibly pay back in five years.

My people are destroyed for lack of knowledge (Hosea 4:6) ran through my mind as I gave Adam some advice. He had not been destroyed through wrongdoing, but simply through his own ignorance. He and his family were about to pay a high price for that lack of knowledge.

There is an interesting dynamic here. If God stands by and allows people to be destroyed through their lack of knowledge, whose responsibility is it to gain that knowledge? Is it God's or ours? The answer is obvious. It is our job to acquire knowledge, not God's job to divinely impart it to us. God would not stand by and watch us perish through lack of knowledge if it were His responsibility to give it to us. It is our responsibility, and we must grasp it. Yet so many of us, in subtle ways, blame God for our financial situations. We resent Him for not supernaturally intervening on our behalf and delivering us from the hole into which we have managed to get ourselves.

We have all heard the saying, "What I don't know can't hurt me." How wrong that is! What we don't know cannot only hurt us, but it can destroy us.

Knowledge is power, and ignorance is debilitating. God has never put His stamp of approval on ignorance. It is disastrous to approach wealth-building from the standpoint of ignorance.

Digging For Answers

Often, when I conduct seminars, I ask people to write down a few things they have always wanted to know about finances. They scratch their heads and talk a little among themselves. Within a few minutes, most of them come up with a short list.

Just when they are feeling proud of their questions, I point out to them that they really don't want to know the answer to whatever they've written down. They may be inquisitive about it, but they don't really want to know. Why? Because if they really wanted to know, they would have searched out the answer for themselves prior to this time.

Knowing means that you take the necessary steps, that you are diligent and that you direct your mind to knowing, investigating and seeking wisdom. I like the wording of Ecclesiastes 7:25 in the *King James Bible.* **I applied mine heart to know and to search, and to seek out wisdom....**

The questions the people come up with in my seminars are often good questions, and the answers to them could easily save them hundreds of dollars with very little effort. But many people have not been willing to expend the necessary effort to gain the knowledge that would help them. Every question has an answer. You may find that answer through reading a book or a magazine or through calling a bank or a financial advisor, but there will always be an answer. If you are going to build and maintain wealth, then you must be prepared to dig for those answers.

Putting Answers To Work

Once you have discovered the answer, you must put it into practice. It sounds so basic, but you would be amazed at how many people are perpetually learning, but never seem to be able to change their behavior. They buy notebooks, tapes, books and cassettes and they are ever learning, but they never manage to apply what they have learned. Surely it is better to know a little and put it into action than to know much and practice none of it. True knowledge is information plus application.

I believe it is time for the people of God to get some knowledge about finances. We have an advantage over unbelievers, and we should use it.

The fear of the Lord is the beginning of knowledge; fools despise wisdom and instruction.
Proverbs 1:7

Knowledge begins with the fear of the Lord, and that's the edge Christians have.

Strategize and Plan Ahead

Unfortunately, when it comes to money, non-Christians often appear to have more common sense than most Christians. More often than not, the church fails in providing a good model for making and handling money.

This situation doesn't seem to have changed much since Biblical times. It was Jesus who said, **For the sons of this world are more shrewd in dealing with their own generation than the sons of light** (Luke 16:8). He was talking about money when He made this statement. Let's look at Jesus' remark in context.

A rich man had a manager who was accused of wasting his master's goods. When the manager was given notice that he was going to lose his job, he went to the people who owed money to his master and reduced the record of the amount of their debt. His reasoning was that when he was out of a job, he would have a few people who owed him a favor!

Jesus told this story and then commented:

> **The master commended the dishonest steward for his shrewdness: for the sons of this world are more shrewd in dealing with their own generation than the sons of light.**
>
> **And I tell you, make friends for yourselves by means of unrighteous mammon, so that when it fails they may receive you into the eternal habitations.**
>
> **Luke 16:8,9**

Is Jesus encouraging us to falsify our financial records? No, such an understanding is not validated in scripture. Instead, Jesus was highlighting the shrewdness and foresight of the manager. Here was a man who could see he was about to undergo a dramatic change in circumstances, so he set about making as many preparations as he could. He was strategizing and planning ahead.

Smarter, Not Harder

I'm sure you know people who have worked hard all their lives, and have little to show for it financially. Perhaps you fall into this category. It's natural to want to work hard to earn as much money as possible, but there are only so many hours in a day in which to work. If you are working sixteen hours a day and somebody tells you to work harder, what are you going to do? Work "smarter," not harder. Through activating strategies based upon sound knowledge, you can learn how to make your income serve you much better than it has ever done before.

The first step in getting smart is to set a system in place where you know exactly what your financial situation is, as well as where you want it to be. To do this will take some time and effort on your part. You must be willing to put the time and effort into it. I commit time each day to cultivate my relationship with the Lord, taking time to pray and study the Word. Each day I also take time to concentrate on gaining financial insight and knowledge about my current financial state.

> **Know well the condition of your flocks, and give attention to your herds;**
>
> **For riches do not last for ever; and does a crown endure to all generations?**
>
> **Proverbs 27:23,24**

In Biblical times, *flocks* represented a family's wealth. They were the original stock investment! The writer of Proverbs urges us to know the condition of our wealth. Is it healthy? Is it about to multiply? The reasons we are to concentrate on these things is because riches and authority don't automatically and indefinitely belong to us. If we do not care for them, they will be gone.

Translating this into modern terms, we could ask, "Do you know the state of your bank accounts? Your interest rates? Your credit rating?" To some, this may seem like "overkill." What is the point of spending time to know this when you only have $100 in the bank? Realistically, the less you have, the more you need to watch over it. Don't wait until you have an amount in the bank that you think is worthy of watching over or you may wait for a long time. Concentrate on what you do have now and how you can utilize it most effectively.

You and Your Money

After realizing they have a Biblical mandate to develop their financial affairs, some people employ the services of a financial advisor. They don't feel knowledgeable or confident enough to handle their own financial affairs. But is employing a financial advisor a good idea? Is it better to entrust your financial situation to an expert? In my opinion, no one is going to put as much care, effort and time into managing your money as you are.

By way of example, I want to share some statistics from tax audits. When audited, 30 percent of tax returns prepared by individuals contained errors. However, 40 percent of the tax returns prepared by CPA's contained errors, and 60 percent of those completed by franchised tax preparers contained errors. The expert may have the most technical knowledge, but there is no one as motivated as you are to manage your own money. Any interest a financial advisor has in managing your money is because he makes his money by watching over yours. But you only have a finite amount of money to spread around. If you spend it paying "experts" to watch over it, you won't have that much left for yourself.

You must take charge over *your* financial affairs.

There are many potential sources of good, free financial advice, so look around and see who God has placed in your life to help with advice.

The way of a fool is right in his own eyes, but a wise man listens to advice.
Proverbs 12:15

Are there godly men and women around you who have been successful in watching over their own money? Ask them questions. Most people are willing to share what they know with you. All you have to do is ask them.

There are also some very good books available on finances, both Christian and non-Christian. Search them out in your local library; then purchase the most useful ones as reference tools.

There are also many free publications available on finances. The Internal Revenue Service publishes a number of them and even provides a toll-free number for inquiries. If you want to know something about a loan, call a bank and talk to someone there. Receptionists will often tell you more over the phone than they would if you showed up in person. Don't be afraid to ask. There are people available with tremendous expertise who are paid solely to serve the public.

Find out what resources are available in your area and use them. The public library is also a good source of many excellent magazines and books that cover specific aspects of finance.

Concentrate on gaining knowledge. Wealth cannot be sustained without it.

What Kind of Knowledge?

The knowledge you need to have will fall into two categories: 1) How to increase your money; and 2) How to invest it wisely.

Charles J Givens, in his book, *Wealth Without Risk*, puts it this way: "If you don't expect to win a lottery, and you don't have the option of inheriting vast sums of money, you only have five ways to increase your wealth:

1. Putting yourself to work — Employment.

2. Putting other people to work — Business.

3. Putting your ideas to work — Inventing, marketing and consulting.

4. Putting your money to work — Investing.

5. Putting other people's money to work — Leverage.
You put your own money to work when you invest in:

* Stocks

* Bonds

* Mutual Funds

* Certificates of Deposit

* IRA's

* Treasury Bills

* Company Retirement Programs

You put other people's money to work when you:

* Buy a home with a mortgage

* Use a brokerage firm or mutual fund margin account

* Take an option on a piece of real estate

* Borrow money for your business

* Invest in leveraged limited partnerships

* Borrow the equity in your home to reinvest

* Expect any financial rewards from the use of borrowed capital."[1]

Although all of the items listed previously may not apply to you, you need to accumulate knowledge about them. A man who had made it to the top of his profession once shared his secret with me. "Whenever I was given a job, I always studied what the man over me was doing. That way when he was absent, I could step into his shoes. When his job became vacant, I was the obvious choice. In this manner, I made my way up the ladder one step at a time."

How true this advice is in the financial setting. If you want to move up a step in wealth-building, you must become familiar with what that step involves. Don't try going from the bottom to the top in one leap. Take your first step, become comfortable with it, then study what the next step involves and take it. It won't be long before you will have climbed a long way with a minimum of stress and personal risk. You will even have the confidence to enjoy the climb, and the view from the top is great!

Specific Information

The remainder of this chapter is intended to be a resource of information. It does not contain every scrap of

[1] Givens, Charles J. *Wealth Without Risk,* Simon & Schuster, 1988, pp. 262-263.

information on finances that you will need to know, but it will provide you with some helpful information and hopefully will act as a springboard for further research. Not everything will apply to your situation. Employ the things that apply to you.

Because taxes and insurance are such heavy outlay items for the average American family, I have dealt with them in separate chapters.

Home Loans

People often ask me, ''Should I buy a home?'' Unless you have access to a special housing subsidy, such as low-rent housing through your job or free rent in exchange for other duties, it is wise to invest in a home. Why pay a landlord when you could be paying yourself?

Buying a home is the entry point for many people into the world of equity, principal and amortization. There is a lot to learn, but if you approach the job one step at a time and ask a lot of questions, you will make it.

The first question to ask is: How much interest should I pay on a loan? This varies with the economy, so you must be prepared to put time into research to find the best interest rates and terms to suit your needs. This information has the potential to save thousands and thousands of dollars for you. Look into the alternatives to a bank loan. There are other institutions which make home loans. Check them out. There are first and second mortgage companies, mortgage brokers, brokerage firms and building societies. Currently, many people think a good interest rate on a mortgage is 10 1/2 to 11 percent. However, there are mortgages you can get at 8 7/8 percent, so do your homework. I just refinanced my home at 5 1/4 percent.

Having searched for the best interest rate, the next issue to settle is, ''For what period of time should your mortgage cover?'' Many people never think to ask this question. They assume that a 30-year mortgage will be half the payments of a 15-year mortgage. Think again! The difference between a 15-year and a 30-year mortgage is only about 15 percent in actual payments. Financial institutions will encourage you to take out a loan for thirty years. However, if you calculate it out, for every $50,000 you borrow on a 15-year term, you will save yourself $80,000 in extra payments that you would have had to pay if you had taken the same amount on a 30-year term. That's a lot of money that could be going toward other things.

The third question you will face is: "Should I use an *adjustable rate mortgage* (ARM) or a *fixed rate mortgage* (FRM)?" These terms are self-explanatory. With a fixed rate mortgage, the interest rate remains constant. Many of our parents bought homes this way. When they started out with a FRM, 3 percent was the going interest rate. Over a period of time, as interest rates rose, they were "laughing all the way to the bank," and there was nothing the bank could do about it.

In response to this, adjustable rate mortgages were introduced where the interest rate can vary by either being pegged to an economic indicator like a treasury bill or by an original agreement between you and the mortgager.

Which one is the best for you? Think of it this way. The FRM is a fixed line. If interest rates drop, you would be better off with an ARM. However, if interest rates rise, you are in a good position. If you decide to go with an ARM, make sure there are some cushions in it for you. The first year's interest rate should be less than 2 percent of a FRM, and it should be able to rise no more than 5 percent above the original rate.

What should you do if you are on a FRM and interest rates drop? Is it time to rush out and refinance? First, there are some built-in costs to change your mortgage, the main one being the closing costs. Since closing costs run at 3 to 4 percent, you need to give careful consideration to the matter. Calculate how much your loan repayments would be reduced. For example, let's say it would reduce your repayment by $150 a month. Then calculate the amount it would cost you in closing costs, let's say $3,600 in this case.

All you have to do now is divide the $3,600 by $150 to calculate how many months it would take you before any savings began to work for you.

In this example, it would be 24 months. Is it worth it? The main consideration is how long you intend to own the house. If you will still be paying off the mortgage in two years, then probably it's worth it. If you plan to sell the house before the two years are up, then it's not worth it. You will have paid out the closing costs but will not have enjoyed the benefits. In general, it is a good idea to refinance when interest rates have dropped at least 2 percent.

Strategies For Paying Back Mortgages

When it comes to a mortgage, you do not have to spend big money to save big money. A little investment can yield surprising results. There are four simple strategies which will save you money and cut years off of your mortgage. Not all banks and lending institutions offer the opportunities these strategies are based upon, so be sure you read the fine print before you sign up for a loan.

For the purpose of the examples that follow, we will assume a 30-year mortgage of $100,000, taken out at 12 percent.

First Day Payment

On the same day as you sign for your mortgage, make your first payment. This will insure that all of your payment is applied toward the principal. This may not seem very startling, but look at what happens if you pay just one month's payment on the first day.

Your first payment would be $1,028. You would cut two years and seven months off your mortgage period, repaying it in under 28 years and saving yourself a total of $31,868. Using the same criteria, were you to pay five months worth of payments, $5,140, you would save $100,834 and reduce your payments by nine years.

As you can see, by using the first-day payment strategy, you can save a lot of money. This occurs because such a large proportion of the initial payments go toward interest. In fact, of your initial payment of $1,028, only $16 is applied to the principal.

Split Payment

Pay half of your monthly mortgage payments every two weeks instead of once a month. This works on two fronts. First, over the course of a year, you will make one extra month's payment since there are 52 weeks in a year, or 26 two-week periods, which in turn is 13 four-week periods, as opposed to 12 monthly periods. Second, splitting the payment means that your principal is being reduced every two weeks instead of only once a month.

One Percent Annual Increase

This strategy requires discipline, but again it is quite simple. Nearly everyone will continue to earn more money each year, and because of that can afford to add 1 percent to their interest payments each year. When you have done this ten times, you will have saved yourself $158,774, and taken 17 years off of your mortgage period.

Extra Payments Using
The Amortized Schedule

For this strategy, you need to have an amortization schedule printed, which tells you what proportion of each payment goes to the principal and which portion goes to interest. When you pay the monthly principal and interest payments on your mortgage, add on to your payment the amount of next month's principal. By doing this each month, you will move through the remaining payment schedule at twice the pace. This is because once you have paid the interest for that month, any extra you put in goes toward paying the amount you actually owe.

Combine the Strategies

Each one of these strategies has tremendous potential. Imagine what using a combination of them would do. Were you to use the first day payment, the split payment and increase your payments 1 percent per year, you would reduce your mortgage from 30 years to 8 years!

John Avanzini, in his immensely practical book, "Rapid Debt Reduction Strategies,"[2] goes into much detail on these points. I would recommend his book, particularly if you want to compare the relative value of specific strategies. He provides over fifty pages of charts on the strategies mentioned previously.

Other People's Money

There are only two sources of money that you can use: your own or *other people's money* (OPM). Knowing when to use each one is a tremendous advantage in wealth building. There are many ways to use OPM successfully. One way is a home equity loan. The aim of many people who pay off their mortgage as quickly as possible is the mental security of a freehold home. In actual fact, investing the equity you have in your home elsewhere is a much smarter idea. You can borrow between 70 to 90 percent of the equity you have in your home.

David and Josie came to one of my seminars on wealth-building. When they returned home after the seminar, they spent some time evaluating. Their main asset was equity in their home, which ran at about $40,000. After some study and prayer, they decided to take out a loan against that equity. With the money, they bought a rental property, for which they paid $15,000 below market value. After making some cosmetic improvements to the home, they re-financed the property to recoup the downpayment and cover their additional costs.

---

[2]Avanzini, John. *Rapid Debt Reduction Strategies*, His Publishing House, 1990.

Within a year of making the choice to use OPM, they had first recovered the money they initially borrowed for the outlay. Second, they owned a rental property, which, incidentally, maintained a positive monthly cash flow for them. Third, once more they had equity to repeat the procedure again, as God directed. All of this was achieved without any "extra" cash of their own.

Using OPM may require a change of mindset for you. Many of us were raised to believe, "If you can't pay cash for it, don't buy it." Using OPM is about as far from that as you can get. There are some risks involved, but if you do your homework and apply the necessary knowledge and discipline and seek God's direction, it can be the shortest way to a new level of independence for you and your family.

OPM can work for you in many other ways as well. Take for example an IRA. It is often a good idea to borrow money for an IRA, because you actually make money by doing so. IRA's are tax-deductible. Let's say you are in the 28 percent tax bracket. You borrow $2,000, (the yearly limit) at 12 percent interest and start an IRA. Since this money is tax-deductible, you will be getting a 28 percent deduction for it versus the 12 percent interest you will pay, leaving you with a net gain.

Asset Management Accounts

Would you like to be able to write checks, or use your credit card while at the same time making 6 to 18 percent interest? The way to do it is with an *Asset Management Account* (AMA). These accounts are available through large financial institutions such as brokerage firms. You can find them in the Yellow Pages under Finance. Call them and ask them to send you a prospectus and answer any questions you have. To open an AMA, you make a deposit into the account. Depending on the institution, you will be required to make an initial deposit anywhere between zero and $25,000, and minimum required account balances fall between zero and $10,000.

Once you have established your account, you will be able to withdraw money from it either by check, Visa card, or American Express card. The card is not technically a credit card, even though the vender you give it to will never be able to tell the difference. It is, in reality, a debit card since you have already deposited the money in the account to cover the outlay. To use the card to its best advantage, calculate the amount you are likely to spend using checks or the debit card for the next month, and deposit that amount into your AMA at the beginning of the month. Your money is then earning interest until the time you spend it, and it is deducted from your account. Once you have made the initial deposit, you are in effect borrowing your own money. That initial $500 or so that you lay out to start the account will literally save you thousands of dollars over the years. It will eliminate the need to use your other expensive credit cards.

You're probably wondering how it is that an AMA can offer such high interest rates. To do it, they use variable interest rates and make additional interest by compounding the rate daily. On top of this, you can choose an account which offers the benefits of a legal float.

Large businesses use a legal float to make millions of dollars. When they need to write a check, their computer will work out the longest distance the check can travel between its origin and its destination. For example, if a company owes somebody money in Connecticut, they will write a check from California and mail it to Connecticut, knowing that it will take four or five days to get there. The money is still in the account those four to five days and is called legal float. Although the money has been legally "paid out," it remains in the bank until the check reaches its destination and is drawn. If enough money is involved, millions of dollars can be made this way. Legal float, though, can work for you on a much smaller scale. Choose an AMA which is processed across the country, thus giving you up to two weeks of "free" money on which to earn interest.

Credit Cards

Credit cards do have a use in your personal wealth-building plan. Keep them as a back-up for insurance purposes. For example, when you insure your car, go for a higher deductible than you normally would. If you raise the deductible $500, you will reduce your comprehensive and collision premiums by 20 to 30 percent. Then, if you do have an accident, you can use your credit card to pay the deductible. Since less than 10 percent of cars each year are involved in insurance claims, there is a good chance you will never have to use this credit loan. In the meantime, you have saved yourself hundreds of dollars in premium payments.

Practical Knowledge

I think you can now see that knowledge used to its fullest advantage can save you money and make you money.

However, it is more than just financial knowledge that can save you money. Proverbs 10:14 says, **Wise men lay up knowledge.** Why? Because any form of knowledge can save or make you money. Simply knowing the best price you can get on a leather jacket will help you decide whether you really are getting a bargain at the "discount" leather store. This kind of knowledge has tangible results.

My wife has purchased shoes that were originally priced between $200 to $300 for as little as $10. Over the years, such purchases have allowed her to enjoy quality goods while at the same time saving literally thousands of dollars.

Think also of the money you could save through a knowledge of how to fix your own car or make your own furniture. Nutritional information can keep you and your family out of the doctor or dentist's office. Tax knowledge can save you the price of a tax preparer. Real estate knowledge can help you select the best home for your money. Electrical knowledge can help you find the fuse which needs to be replaced instead of having to call a repairman. Computer knowledge can help you select the most suitable program for your needs. There is literally no end to the advantages you can give yourself by ''storing up knowledge.''

There is so much to learn, but the Holy Spirit will ''bring all things to your remembrance.'' That means *all things.* If we are diligent to fill our minds with knowledge, God promises to release it to us as we need it. I have had things stored up in my mind for years, and when I have needed that knowledge, the Holy Spirit has helped me to recall it and use it. If I had not put it into my mind in the first place, however, the Holy Spirit could not have helped me recall it.

How many of you look back on your school years and see knowledge that would be a wonderful help to you now if only you had concentrated on it more back then? If God puts you in a situation where you can learn anything about any area, do it. You will later regret it if you don't. Whether it is about the causes of respiratory diseases or 21 games preschoolers love, store up that knowledge. God holds your future in His hands. Don't let opportunities to gain knowledge slip through your hands. Instead, value all forms of knowledge.

Every day I attempt to learn something new about finances. I do it, not because I want to become a financial whiz, but because that knowledge will help me save money at some point in my life. Hardly a week goes by where I don't see some tangible results from the knowledge I have gained.

> **A wise man is mightier than a strong man, and a man of knowledge than he who has strength.**
> **Proverbs 24:5**

4
Record-Keeping

"Just get in the car and wait for me, and quit annoying each other," Beth yelled frustratedly at her children, while continuing her search. She had rummaged through the pile of papers on top of the refrigerator, checked the table behind the couch and looked through her bureau drawer. Where could Joe's immunization records possibly be? Of course, they were probably mixed in with her mounting pile of unanswered correspondence. She flicked through it, but to no avail. It wasn't there.

Beth's anger and frustration grew. Why hadn't she been more careful with them? Today was the last day they could be submitted. Joe would not be allowed to attend any more school until his immunization records were produced. Where could those records be?

The same scenario is replayed daily in countless homes across the nation. The object lost may be different, but the desperate hunt is the same. In one home, it could be college transcripts needed to apply for a new job. In another, plumbing diagrams to locate the leaking pipe under the floor. In still another, lost receipts for tax-deductible items.

Most families suffer from a lack of orderly record-keeping, which causes high levels of stress. Lost records mean lost time, money and opportunities.

But if you want to become serious about wealth-building, then you must become serious about record-keeping. Everyone has records of one kind or another. Would you be able to find the electric bill you paid in March

43

of 1990? What about your rent stubs for 1988? Are they buried with piles of other papers in a box under your bed?

The Greatest Record Keeper

God is the greatest record keeper ever. He had 45 secretaries for over 1,500 years documenting everything He did. Compiled together, those records became the Bible. From Genesis to Revelation, God continually recorded facts and insights so they wouldn't be lost. These diligently-kept records form the basis of the Christian faith.

Consider the Ten Commandments.

And Moses turned, and went down from the mountain with the two tables of the testimony in his hands, tables that were written on both sides; on the one side and on the other were they written.

And tables were the work of God, and the writing was the writing of God, graven upon the tables.
Exodus 32:15,16

God Himself did the recording on the stone tables He gave to Moses. They were given in that form so they would be a tangible record of how God expected men to live.

Inasmuch as many have undertaken to compile a narrative of the things which have been accomplished among us,

Just as they were delivered to us by those who from the beginning were eyewitnesses and ministers of the word,

It seemed good to me also, having followed all things closely for some time past, to write an orderly account for you, most excellent Theophilus,

That you may know the truth concerning the things of which you have been informed.
Luke 1:1-4

With this introduction, Luke produced the most thorough account of Jesus' life that we have. Luke assumed Theophilus had already heard most of the stories that would be told in his account, but he wanted to write them down in an *orderly* manner which would enable Theophilus to trace the truth of the events as they unfolded.

This idea of record-keeping is also found in Revelation.

The revelation of Jesus Christ, which God gave him to show to his servants what must soon take place; and he made it known by sending his angel to his servant John,

Who bore witness to the word of God and to the testimony of Jesus Christ, even to all he saw.

Revelation 1:1,2

How did John bear witness? How did he make permanent that which he had seen? In Revelation 1:11, he gives us the answer: **Write what you see in a book and send it to the seven churches.** John already had a relationship with the seven churches. He could just as easily have delivered the vision to them orally. But God instructed him to write it in a book.

As we read through the Bible, we become aware that every covenant, every promise, every law is recorded in writing. We can't say, "Sorry, God, I thought You said...." No, God has documented everything He said to us. He leaves nothing to chance. Everything is carefully written for all to see and understand what He meant.

Be Imitators of God

Each person needs to ask, "Am I imitating God in this way?" Get serious about documenting and record-keeping. Not only will you be imitating the Lord, but accurate record-keeping will also provide three things for you: a good reputation, peace of mind and more money.

Poor Record-Keeping Can Ruin You

Several years ago, I started a new church in Cortland, Ohio. At first, the church did not have a very well-established name, and as a result, most people came to know the church as "Luther Blackwell's Church." Because of this, many people wrote their offering checks out in my name. No one thought much about it. I processed the checks through my account, then transferred the money to the church account. If you know anything about finances, I'm sure you are hearing warning bells already!

All went smoothly until I filed my tax return and received an audit notice. I was shocked to discover that the way I had processed the money made it look as though I had embezzled church funds. Embezzlement means big trouble with the IRS and the law. It was a grueling, time-consuming process, but thank God, I was able to produce a paper trail of where the income had come from and where it went that eventually satisfied the IRS.

It was a gut-wrenching experience, and one I don't want to repeat. All that stood between my good name and a ruined reputation was documentation. But I learned my lesson well. Never again have I processed money thoughtlessly, under any circumstances, and I make sure everything I do is clearly documented.

Can You Find It When You Need It?

Without good record-keeping, you will experience considerably more stress in your life. There will be unexpected times when you have to produce records and documents. If they have not been kept or they cannot be found, the consequences can be serious.

Doug worked for a multi-national company and had just received a big job promotion. Accepting the promotion meant Doug and his family would have to move from their home in Toronto, Canada, to Chicago. One of Doug's three children was Kim, a South Korean girl, whom they had adopted as a baby.

With the aid of the company attorney, Doug filled out all the necessary paperwork to apply for a work visa to the United States. In addition to all of the forms, he had to produce a number of records: bank statements, marriage certificate, birth certificates for his children, college transcripts and more. It took searching through many boxes and piles of personal papers, but finally, Doug located everything he needed except Kim's birth certificate. He knew he had it somewhere, but he just couldn't find it.

Finally, there was no option but to send to South Korea for a duplicate copy. The bureaucrats in South Korea were not impressed with the urgency of Doug's request, and it was four months before the duplicate certificate arrived. The delay caused unnecessary holdups and frustration, and Doug finally arrived in Chicago six months after the date he was supposed to have started his new job.

Some simple organization of the family's personal papers would have saved Doug and his family much personal anguish.

What Kind of System?

People often ask me, ''What is the best kind of record-keeping system?'' You can go to an office supply store and buy yourself an expensive filing system, but for most people, that is not necessary in the beginning. All you really need is a logical system and a secure place to keep it. It can be as simple as a cardboard box with file folders in it. One hundred file folders will cost you about $3 at a discount office supply store, and you can label them to suit your needs. At a later time, when you have made room for it in your budget, you can transfer them into a file cabinet. The important thing is not how elegant the system looks. It's how useful it is to you.

Accurate Records Will Save You Money

Most families lose hundreds of dollars a year simply because they fail to keep complete records. This is especially true in the area of taxes, where the greatest single proportion of the average family's income goes. Those individuals who have the discipline and vision to keep good and accurate records are the ones who will end up paying less in taxes. If you want a tax refund or deduction for things you have purchased, you need good records.

Record-keeping may seem like a lot of extra trouble to you at first, but as you become more skilled at it, it will become second nature. God takes pleasure in documentation, and He will take pleasure in you when you imitate Him in this area.

In setting your house in order, you must set your records straight. Regardless of the disorder they may be in, with a little discipline, you can organize them. And when you have done it, you will discover that accurate records really do pay off.

5

Taxes

Ernest and Debbie Greene could feel the tension rising. Debbie found herself getting more and more irritable with the children, and Ernest found himself avoiding home and spending more time at the office than was needed. It was August, and instead of having the tax hurdle behind, it loomed larger than ever before them.

They had already applied for one extension on filing their tax returns, so Debbie tried again. The IRS told her she would have to supply a verifiable reason for wanting the extension, something like moving from one state to another, or the recent death of a family member. Procrastination, unfortunately, was not a verifiable excuse. They hadn't been able to decide if it was better for them to file separately or jointly. Losing a paper sack full of tax-deductible receipts only complicated the matter. Their disorganization and lack of knowledge had worked them into a tight corner, and they were unsure how to get themselves out of it.

Ernest and Debbie came to see me, and I suggested to them that they make the seven changes outlined below. By doing so, they would ensure never ending up in the same depressing situation again.

Plan Ahead, Not Behind

Plan behind? How can you do that? I don't know, but millions of people try to do it every year! They wait till their tax returns are due, and then they try to work out a strategy for the past tax year. Invariably, they discover they haven't kept the correct paperwork, and they have made some fundamental mistakes that it's too late to correct.

As basic as it may seem, you have to stop reacting to the year that has already passed, and make the mental switch to controlling your current tax year. Plan ahead. Keep your receipts well organized. Study the situation. See where you can make tax savings. Keep on top of things. When April comes, it is then simply a matter of collecting the relevant pieces of information together and arranging them in an orderly fashion to present to the IRS. You know exactly what you have claimed and why, so there is little or no stress — just a pile of forms to fill out.

Getting to this place of being in control of your tax year means dealing with the human propensity to procrastinate. You need a new mindset, a mindset where you plan a specific time each week to go over your finances and plan ahead.

Keep Impeccable Records

There is no other area I can think of where keeping orderly records is of such obvious financial benefit. You need to have records that will prove and document everything you want to deduct from your taxes.

Record-keeping need not be complex, but it must be thorough. Over the years, I have found the following system to be the most successful and painless. I keep a large four-inch thick folder on my desk. I divide it into various sections, depending upon my financial state. At present, I have sections for Rental Properties, Pastoral Travel, Amplified Productions (my worship music business) Travel, Investments, Insurance, Interest Payments and several others.

When I'm given a receipt for payment of something I want to claim on my taxes, I photocopy it, and file the photocopied receipt in the relevant section of the folder. I make sure that the date, a description of the item, and the category it will be claimed under are recorded on the page. For instance, "5/7/91, $12.50, File Folders, Amplified Office Equipment," or "4/3/91, $9,000, Reroofing 199 Alm Lane, Labor and Materials, Rental Property Upgrade." By doing this, neither I nor anyone else will have a doubt as to why the receipt has been kept.

Although photocopying receipts is initially a bother, it is well worth the effort. Through experience, I have found that receipts come in so many shapes and sizes that it is nearly impossible to keep them in any type of reasonable order. I store the original receipts in a box, marked with the date. That way I know where to find them if I am asked to produce them.

When I took the folder to my CPA, he laughed. "This is a tax man's nightmare. You have everything tied down so tightly, he wouldn't have room to object to anything! If you show this to the IRS, they will back right away from you," he told me.

You can end your tax year with the same confidence. All it takes is about $20 worth of materials and some discipline.

Be Prepared to Answer Questions

It is easy to get a little defensive about having to produce so many specific documents to prove things. But the IRS has a right to query any expense we list in our tax returns. It is their business. They are a federal agency charged with ensuring that tax fraud and evasion do not occur. How are they going to do this unless they have the right to investigate?

It is a matter of principle, not an invasion of our privacy, that we are able to verify what we have claimed. Before Paul visited the Corinthian Christians, he told them he would only listen to charges which were verified. **Any charge must be sustained by the evidence of two or three witnesses** (2 Corinthians 13:1). Our records are a witness to the truth of what we have said.

Many people have an uninformed fear of being audited. They don't want to claim anything unusual because it might draw extra attention to themselves. This is not the case. Auditing selections are made by a computer. It selects a prearranged number of individuals and businesses within each category. Approximately 2 percent of all small businesses (incomes between $10,000 and $30,000) and the same percentage of individuals earning under $50,000 are audited. Judging by these statistics, you will probably be audited once or twice in your lifetime. Don't fear an audit. Instead, do your homework well in advance, and there will be no cause for distress.

On the other hand, no one wants to go through the extra expense and inconvenience of an audit. The best way to reduce your chances is to file your return as late as possible. Fill your tax return out at the normal time, but apply for an automatic extension until August 15. Ask for Automatic Extension Form 4868.

Keep Up To Date

Betty Johnson has her family well trained. Whenever they buy anything, they save the receipt and lodge it in the large, cardboard box beside Betty's desk. On the last day of every month, Betty takes them all out, circles the sales tax component and tallies the total. Then, at the end of the tax year, she totals the twelve months and claims the amount as a deduction on her income tax. I admire her organization and tenacity. Unfortunately, it is misdirected. In 1987, Congress canceled any deductions allowed on the sales tax of personal purchases.

Tax laws are in a state of constant change. Some changes, like the sales tax deduction, can be relatively harmless. All it cost Betty Johnson was her time, some eye strain and a hurt ego when a friend finally pointed the error out to her.

Other tax law changes can cost us much more, either in money we did not know we could claim, or in adjustments we could have made in tax strategies. The best way to keep abreast of these changes is to research. Tax preparing companies and the IRS give out free information. Read this material. If it doesn't make sense to you, ask questions and keep on asking questions until it does.

An excellent book on the topic is Sylvia Porter's *385 Tax-Saving Tips*.[3] It is exactly that — 385 ways to legitimately save on taxes. Her categories range from medical expenses through real estate to the "best" time to have a baby! I guarantee you will learn something that will save you money.

Don't Take the Easy Way Out

People often hurry into filling out and filing the short tax form. They rationalize that it is much simpler and will yield the same results as filing the long form. Unfortunately, this is not true. It is the diligent, not the lazy, who make wealth.

In choosing the short form, you are choosing to overlook possibly hundreds or thousands of dollars worth of deductions. How will you ever know what deductions you could be eligible to claim, unless you take the effort to fill out the long form?

Even if filing the long form doesn't save you vast amounts in the first year, it will acquaint you with many ways to document and save the next time around. Talk yourself out of the idea of taking the quick way. What you don't know will always cost you.

Aim High

Most tax experts maintain that no one needs to pay out more than 5 percent of their income in taxes. How much tax are you paying at present? Most likely, you are in the 28 percent bracket. Most wealthy people are in the 33 percent bracket, yet manage to pay very little tax. Why is

---

[3] Porter, Sylvia. *385 Tax-Saving Tips*, Avon Books, 1990.

this? It is due, in part, to the fact that tax laws, being made and passed by rich people, are slanted unfairly against the middle and lower classes. But it is also true that wealthy people are well aware of the tax system and utilize it to their advantage. If you want to drastically reduce your tax load, then you need to do the same.

But what about the ethics of reducing your taxes? Isn't there a social obligation to pay Uncle Sam? After all, if there were no taxes, who would fund the homeless shelters, schools, Medicare, etc.? Regardless of this, you are under no obligation to pay any more tax than you legally owe.

Porter puts it succinctly, "Remember what Justice Learned Hand said: Tax avoidance isn't the same as tax evasion. You can do everything within your power to lower your taxes, by legitimate means."[4]

You are not under any legal or ethical obligation to pay more than the law requires of you. The advantage of paying less taxes is that you can exercise direct control over where your money goes. Instead of it being applied to secular social service programs, you have the liberty to give it to a Christian counterpart.

By using the power of knowledge and discipline, you should be able to reduce your taxes to between 5 and 8 percent. Take it as a challenge. If countless others can do it, so can you!

Know Your Deductions

Owning a business offers a large variety of tax deductions and is well worth investigating. Of all the tax strategies I could share, this is probably the most useful to the greatest number of people. What kind of business should you start? It could be anything — from cheese making to singing at weddings.

---

[4]*Ibid.*, p. 3.

Take some time to review your talents and hobbies. (See the section, "The God Of Opportunities" in chapter 10.) Perhaps you like to bake, or craft wooden toys, or help kids with English, or knit sweaters, or fix lawn mowers. Any of these, and a myriad of other activities, can form the basis of a successful small business.

What makes something a business rather than a hobby? In the eyes of the IRS, it is the intent to make money by selling a service or goods to the public. (A hobby may have income as a by-product, but the intention is enjoyment.) How do you show that you intend to make money? You need to open a separate bank account, give your business a name, keep an account of income and expenses and have a record of potential or actual customers with whom you keep in contact in some way. It is also useful to have some written form of communication about your goods or service. Posters, business cards, fliers and the like are good.

Remember, it is the *intent* to make a profit, not the profit itself, which is the criteria. Thousands of businesses operate in the red every day.

The easiest way to start a small business is as a "sole proprietorship," thereby allowing you to use your social security number as a tax identification number.

Once you have begun a small business, there are a number of tax deductions for which you may immediately be eligible. The most popular of these deductions are:

1. Videos and book subscriptions.

2. Your home, if you have an office there.

3. Your telephone, fax machine, computer and other pieces of equipment used in your business.

4. Your car, mileage, and an RV or other form of transportation, such as a boat or airplane.

5. Interest on the asset loans of your business.

6. Employ your children or parents. (You can pay up to $3,000 a year and still claim dependency allowances.)

7. Travel, combining business and pleasure.

8. Continuing education, seminars, etc.

9. Club memberships.

The list could go on and on. There are many obscure deductions to which you may be entitled. For a comprehensive look at these deductions, get a copy of the ''Tax Guide For Small Businesses,'' Publication 334, from your local IRS office. If you still have questions, ask someone. There is no reason why you and your family should not join the thousands of other families in the United States who are taking advantage of these opportunities.

By implementing these seven tax strategies, you will be in control of your tax situation. Income taxes and the IRS are not something to be feared. With wise planning, you should be able to significantly reduce the amount of tax you pay each year, and less tax means more money for you to use in building your wealth.

6
Insurance

It may sound paradoxical, but in the process of wealth-building, you need to anticipate unforeseen circumstances. We all have nagging fears: What if my house is broken into while I'm on vacation? What if I total someone's Mercedes-Benz Coupe 500 with my cheap car? What if my spouse dies before the house is paid for? What if I need long-term hospital care?

These are legitimate situations that could very easily happen to us in the course of life, and some provision needs to be made for them on our part. The best way to make such provision is through insurance. Insurance is designed to provide us with peace of mind, minimizing the financial effect of these situations should they occur.

However, the insurance industry is also designed to take our money at every turn. Insurance companies are not charitable institutions. They run on profits. They will provide peace of mind, but their peace of mind has a price tag. Thus, we must become savvy and learn to use insurance to our advantage. Let's look at some specific types of insurance to see how it can work to our advantage.

Life Insurance

Most people need life insurance of some type. Ironically, the times when people need it the most, they tend to have it the least. This is because they have not really thought through the reasons for having life insurance and assessed their own situation.

One important fact to fix firmly in your mind about life insurance is that *you* will never benefit from it. Life insurance is designed to be paid upon your death to whomever you choose to leave it. This means your sole reason for buying life insurance is to protect the financial security of those you leave behind.

It stands to reason, then, that you need life insurance if:

1. Other people are dependent upon your income, such as a spouse or children.

2. You render a service which would have to be paid for by another individual if you were to die.

In many families with young children, the husband carries life insurance because he is the breadwinner. However, were his wife to die, he could be in serious financial trouble. Suddenly, he would be faced with the cost of long-term day care (including vacation times) and housekeeping bills. When you are assessing insurance needs, it pays to think in terms of *duties carried out* as well as income brought in.

Using this method, you can see there is little point in a single person being insured, unless, for example, an elderly parent is dependent upon them for care. In that case, they may want to carry insurance until the parent dies. You can also see that life insurance for children is a complete waste of money. Beyond paying funeral expenses, how is a child's death going to cause financial hardship for the survivors? Resist the insurance agent who says, ''If you love your child, you will insure them.'' It isn't true.

Of course, you should carry the most life insurance when: 1) You have the most people financially dependent upon you, and 2) When the most hardship would be caused without your paycheck. It sounds simple, and it is. In nearly every case, you should carry maximum insurance when your children are small and decrease it as they get nearer to financial independence. This normally coincides with you building more assets and equity in your home as well.

There should come a time when you no longer require life insurance, where you have planned and invested enough, so that if you were to die, provision would be made for your dependents.

Whole Life Insurance

There are three fundamental categories of life insurance. The first and most common category includes *universal* or *whole life insurance.*

Universal insurance is billed as a great investment plan, but it is flawed. Commissions and fees are deducted off the top end of the premium before the interest on your "investment" is calculated. These "incidental" costs can lower the premium by as much as 30 percent. That means you have just rendered 30 percent of your premium useless to you. Policies also guarantee interest rates of 10 percent, which is not too bad until you consider that it is only for the first year. After that, the interest rate can plummet to below 5 percent. When you finally realize that you are losing money this way and want to bail out, you are hit again. Most of these kinds of policies require large surrender fees.

Never use life insurance as an investment. It never has been and never will be an investment. If you want to invest money, do it deliberately and intelligently. Universal insurance exists solely for the individual who is too lazy to research and wants to dump money into a "no thought required" account.

Whole life insurance also has its pitfalls. Whole life insurers try to attract you with three major claims. Let's look at each of them:

1. *Level premiums.* This means the premiums do not rise over time. This appeals greatly to human nature. Who doesn't want to pay into something which is guaranteed to remain constant? Other insurance premiums increase, but this one doesn't. There is good reason for this. The only way an offer like this can be made is to artificially inflate

the initial premium payments to cover the cost of the later ones. The younger you die, the more you lose.

2. *You can borrow your cash value.* The cash value is the amount *you* have already paid into the account, not the amount your heirs will collect. So for about 7 percent interest, you have the privilege of borrowing your own money. That doesn't sound like a wonderful deal to me!

3. *High interest rates.* Although insurance companies claim this, in actual fact, when all factors are taken into consideration, the interest rate is normally under 2 percent. In addition, unless you live to an old age, no one will ever see that interest. Why? Read on.

With a whole life policy, the insurance company pays out what is known as a *lump sum payout of death benefits* upon your death. You would expect your heirs to receive the cash value (what you have paid into the policy), plus the amount of the policy you opted for. Although most policy owners don't know it, this is simply not the case. You get either the cash value *or* the initial policy value, but not both. Since the meager interest you earn is added to the policy's cash value, unless the cash value exceeds the policy value, it will be absorbed by the insurance company.

Let's say, for example, you buy a $200,000 whole life policy and pay $2,000 into it each year. If you were to die 15 years later, you have paid $30,000 into the policy. Your 2 percent interest would be added to that cash value. Remember, it is an either/or proposition. You get to choose either the $30,000 plus 2 percent interest *or* the $200,000, a fairly easy choice. The premiums which you "invested" all go to the insurance company, along with the interest from them. At least the "investor" is not around to see the results of his efforts, or to calculate how much his heirs could have if he had invested the $30,000 in a safe investment plan at about 20 percent.

If you don't use your head when buying life insurance, you will lose every time. Insurers count on their clients accepting their word, and it works. Insurance companies get richer every year, "helping" you out of your money in the process.

Single Premium Whole Life

The second category of life insurance is called *single premium whole life insurance*. As the name implies, the client makes one single deposit against a whole life policy. Of course, the payment is going to be a large amount. These types of policies are normally bought by people who use them for tax-shelter purposes. However, there are much better tax shelters if you research. For example, tax-sheltered annuities are a much better investment. There is basically no logical reason for using this type of insurance.

Term Life Insurance

The third category of life insurance is the least known and least used of the three. It is also the least publicized by insurance companies. It is *term life insurance*.

As the name implies, you are buying insurance for a specific period of time. You can choose a policy for which the premiums rise slowly but steadily each year. This is called an Annually Renewable Term (ART) policy. Or you may choose a Level Premium Term (LPT) policy in which the premium stays at a constant rate throughout the term you own the policy.

The beauty of term insurance is twofold. First, you buy what you need to cover yourself at any given time in your life. For instance, when you purchase a home, instead of buying credit life insurance on your mortgage, take out the same amount in term insurance. With credit life insurance, the amount paid out declines from the day you purchase it. In addition, it never goes to your heirs, but to the company financing your loan. By taking out term life insurance, if you died within the term of the insurance policy, your heirs would receive the entire amount. Then they would be able to invest the payout, make the mortgage payments with the interest, and end up with a paid-off house and the entire capital to reinvest.

The second advantage of term insurance is that it is much cheaper than whole life insurance. Ask for comparative charts from your insurance agent. He may grimace, but he will give them to you. In the charts, you will find that you can buy $100,000 worth of ART coverage for as little as $150 in the first year (based on figures for a 40-year-old man). As I pointed out, it will rise as you become older and therefore become more of a risk. But even ten years later, the same insurance would have only risen to $190 a year. It almost sounds too good to be true. Check it out for yourself. Term life insurance is the insurance industries' best-kept secret!

Auto Insurance

There are nine major categories of auto insurance and innumerable subcategories. It is no wonder people become confused! The most useful overall reference I have seen regarding auto insurance is found in Charles J. Given's book, *Wealth Without Risk*. I have drawn heavily on it for the information presented in this section.

Space does not permit a thorough rendering of every facet of auto insurance, so once you have a general idea of what you are looking for, I would suggest you study specific aspects more fully.

Basically, most car owners will find themselves needing several of the following categories of auto insurance:

Bodily Injury Liability

This covers injury to people, the passengers in your car, people in another car in the case of a collision and pedestrians. You and your family members are also covered if you are injured in someone else's car or in a rental car. It also covers legal costs up to the level of the policy. Normally, the policy has two limits: the ceiling amount paid out on any one person, and the total amount paid out on any one accident. It is expressed like this: $10,000/$20,000 ($10,000 per person, $20,000 per accident).

You probably already have this type of insurance since it is required by law in most states. How much bodily injury liability insurance you should carry depends primarily on how much you own. The more assets you have, the more for which you can be sued. As a rule of thumb, buy one-and-a-third to one-and-a-half times the net value of your assets.

Property Damage

This insurance pays out for any damage your car causes to another car or person's property, such as a house or fence. Of course, it only pays out up to the limit of the policy. Other family members, and people with permission to drive your car, are also covered.

Unfortunately, the potential damage you could do is astronomical. To reach a policy amount, you need to weigh the probability of an expensive accident against the cost of the policy. You should carry, at a minimum, $50,000 worth of property damage insurance.

Collision Insurance

As the name suggests, this covers your vehicle in the event of a collision. You pay the deductible, but if the other driver is at fault, then your insurance company will collect the money from that driver's insurance company and reimburse your deductible.

Comprehensive Insurance

This insurance covers damage to your car which is not caused by an accident. Your imagination can run wild here! Some examples are falling trees, power lines, attempted break-ins and actual theft, hail pockmarks and shattered windshields.

Whether you should carry comprehensive or collision insurance is determined by the cost of repairing or replacing your car. You cannot claim more than the car is worth, so there is no use paying high premiums on a 1978 Chevrolet.

In fact, once a car dips below $2,000 in value, it is not worth carrying these two types of insurance at all.

No-Fault Insurance

No-fault insurance allows you to collect insurance without the legal costs and inconvenience of proving fault. It covers such things as medical expenses, loss of income, property damage, compensation for death and permanent injury. However, it is also a duplicate form of insurance and not really needed unless state law requires you to carry it. Your medical insurance will cover your medical expenses, and property damage is covered by your collision insurance. If you don't need collision insurance, then you don't need no-fault insurance either.

Medical Payments

It is much cheaper to carry separate medical insurance than it is to integrate it into an auto insurance policy.

Death or Dismemberment

This is a variation on medical payments, and for the same reasons, it is not useful.

Uninsured Motorist

This insurance is carried in case the person who does damage to you or your car either cannot be found or has no insurance. For example, you may be injured in a hit-and-run accident, or you may be hurt in an accident with an under-age driver. However, like no-fault insurance, this is a duplicate insurance. Your medical bills will be covered by your medical policy.

No insurance company will compensate you twice for one injury, so it is pointless to carry duplicate insurance.

Emergency Road Service

This insurance covers the cost of towing your car should it break down while you are driving. Statistically, this type of insurance is not worth the cost. Instead, put the extra amount into an investment plan.

These are the various categories of auto insurance. Decide what you need; then shop around for the best price. Call some insurance companies and find out the best deal they can offer you.

Health Insurance

With health insurance, as with any insurance, you need to balance the cost of the premium against the benefits you receive. In the case of medical insurance, about half the premium is paid to insure the first $1,000 to $2,500 of a claim. By raising your deductible to $1,000 or more, you can reduce the amount of your premium by about 50 percent.

Basically, what you need is called "major medical insurance." This type of insurance covers your risk on such health costs as major health problems and chronic illness, accidents and surgery. Take the money you save in reduced premiums and invest it. Then, if the need arises, you have the money to pay for smaller medical bills.

Making Claims

Once you have chosen the appropriate form of insurance, the next question to ask is, "When should I make a claim?" Several years ago, I learned this lesson the hard way. Lightning hit my house and did minor damage to the roof. I thought to myself, "This is why I pay insurance. Let them pay for the repairs." They did, and the bill amounted to about $100. What I didn't consider at the time was that it cost the insurance company around $400 to process that claim, and it went on my insurance record.

Not long afterwards, we had a house fire. It started in the light fixture in my shower and quickly spread through much of the house. It was a terrible shock for my family and me to experience. However, we still had good insurance, and they paid the $180,000 repair bill.

There was just one catch. Soon after the fire, my insurance company notified me that they were not renewing my insurance. I didn't know that the law states that after two claims, a company is not required to reinsure you. I had to search around for another insurance policy on my house, and the premium was several hundred dollars more than I had been paying. Had I known all this before, I would never have claimed the $100 damage from the lightning.

Rather than decline you, other insurance companies automatically increase your premiums when you make a claim, some by as much as 25 percent. Once again, knowledge is the key. It is not just having the right insurance, but it is also knowing when it is and when it isn't appropriate to make a claim.

Shop Around

You have to "shop" around for the best deal with any form of insurance. Amazingly, though, over half of those who buy auto insurance never check with other insurance companies for a comparison. Premium rates can vary up to 100 percent among insurance companies. It is foolish not to check out alternatives before settling for one company, so keep shopping until you get a bargain.

Entire books have been written on the various types of insurance, so it is unrealistic to think that all aspects of insurance have been covered in this chapter. What I have tried to do is give you enough information so that you realize there are many choices available to you. Each choice offers different advantages and disadvantages. It's your job to do some research to find out which choices are the best for you.

7

A Good Name

A good name is to be chosen rather than great riches, and favor is better than silver or gold.
Proverbs 22:1

A name is a very precious commodity in God's eyes. In the very first chapter of the Bible (Genesis 1), Adam is told by God to name the animals. In the Bible's closing chapter (Revelation 22), we are told that we will see God's face, and His name will be written upon our foreheads. Perhaps the importance of having a good name has never occurred to you before, but if you study the scriptures, you will find it is a recurring theme.

One day as I meditated about a good name being more precious than gold or silver, the Lord challenged me to test the validity of this truth. I picked up the phone and called the bank. Over the phone, I asked for a $10,000 loan. The normal personal loan limit is $5,000. The bank representative placed the phone on hold for a few moments while he checked my financial records, and then informed me that I could have the $10,000 in two hours.

Now, I know if I should ever need $10,000 in a hurry, my good name can secure it for me. My good name has the power to provide financial benefits for me.

You will get a good name in your financial dealings by being on time with your payments, by living up to your end of agreements (or contracts) and following through on them. However, if you abuse your credit cards, fail to make payments when they are due, and otherwise mishandle your financial obligations, your good name is going to be severely tarnished, which will affect your ability to get credit for years to come.

Many Christians today do not have a good name and do not have credit available to them simply by virtue of their name.

Our Corporate Name

We need to realize that we are one body in Christ, and what affects one of us affects all of us. We need to maintain good credit, not only for ourselves, but as a witness to those with whom we deal and as a positive reflection upon our brothers and sisters in Christ.

In his excellent book, *Business by the Book,* Larry Burkett recounts a sobering situation:

"Integrity is a rare commodity in our generation, especially where other people's money is concerned. A Christian who wants to have a credible witness needs to meet at least this minimum standard. I recall a note I received in 1976 from the chairman of one of the largest paper companies in America. It simply said, 'Thank you for the integrity you have shown in paying your bills to our company.'

"I thought that was remarkable because our total purchases for the previous year couldn't have been $10,000 — certainly only a fraction of their total sales. So I decided to call the chairman to ask why he wrote the note.

"He said, 'Your ministry is one of the few Christian organizations we deal with that pays its bills on time — every time. I'm a Christian also, but the delinquencies among churches and other ministries have become a source of ridicule in some of the directors' meetings.'

"It is remarkable that the head of a major company would be subjected to ridicule from his peers for the failure of Christian-run organizations to pay their bills on time.

Small wonder that many people avoid doing business with Christians!"[5]

Do others like to do business with you? If you were to apply for a loan, are there certain facts from your previous financial dealings that would be embarrassing and detrimental to your chances if they came to light? As embarrassing as it may be, reality is that many people dig themselves into financial holes. In their attempts to extract themselves from these holes, many people leave their names and reputations in tatters.

Perhaps you are one of these people. Perhaps you have reneged on a loan or had a car repossessed or failed to make your monthly credit card payments and your credit card has been canceled. Now, every time you try to get credit, you come up against a brick wall. There is good news for you. You don't have to settle for this situation. You can redeem your good name. There are ways you can develop a good financial name for yourself, and you will discover what some of these ways are as you read on through this chapter.

Credit Reports

Somewhere in the business world, there is a credit report with your name on it. Anyone who wants to can apply for a copy of it and find out just how good his name really is. Do you know what is in your credit report? Have you ever seen a copy of it? You should make it your business to know what is in your credit report, because nearly 60 percent of all credit reports contain errors. It could be that you have been turned down for credit because of some incorrect information in your credit report. The computer doesn't know there are errors. The only person who can spot the errors is *you*. It is your responsibility to make sure that your name is being presented accurately to the business world.

---

[5]Burkett, Larry. *Business by the Book*, Thomas Nelson Publishers, 1990, p. 23.

To get a copy of your credit report, look in the yellow pages under Credit Bureaus. Call one of them and ask for a copy of your credit report. For a nominal sum of money, they will send a copy of it to you. The credit report comes complete with a key to the abbreviations used in it, so even the novice can make sense of it. Along with the credit report will be a list of every individual or company who has requested a copy of your credit record over the past year. Look the report over carefully. You are looking for two things: any negative record in the report that is incorrect, and any positive credit omissions.

If you find any mistakes or omissions, contact the credit bureau and have them correct your file. They are obliged to do this under law. Even if the negative information is correct, it can only stay on your credit file for seven years, or in the case of bankruptcy, ten years. If there is information lingering past this time frame on your report, ask for it to be immediately removed. On the other hand, perhaps you have successfully made payments or paid off a loan, and they are not recorded on your credit report. They should be, and it is in your interest to make sure that they are recorded. If you provide the details in writing to the credit bureau, they will add them into your records.

Turning Your Credit Around

What do you do if your credit report is bad but accurate? Don't become fatalistic about the situation. Don't sit with your head in your hands and bemoan how you had your chance and blew it, about how you are now going to have to learn to live with the consequences. Give yourself a second chance. Get to work and see what can be done about turning your bad credit around. It is sad to say, but I have found Christians to be some of the most fatalistic and non-assertive people when it comes to dealing with this area. But deal with it and turn it around we must if we are ever going to accumulate wealth.

Before you do anything, you need to understand the root of your bad credit. There is no use re-establishing your credit rating if you can't handle your money any better than you did before. Hopefully, by the time you have finished reading this book, you will be well on your way to becoming a wise financial manager.

There are two steps to restoring bad credit. The first step is accomplished by beginning to outweigh your bad credit with good credit. Get yourself a secured credit card. This is usually a Visa or a MasterCard. You do not need good credit to get one, because you pay the money up front into an account. It works like this: you deposit enough money into a bank account to cover what is being drawn out. The bank is not actually extending you any credit on your "credit" card, because the money is already in the bank.

After several months of maintaining a good record, the bank will usually lift their restrictions and allow you to use real credit with the card. When this happens, contact the credit bureau and have them enter it on your credit report. You are now on your way!

The second step is to take out a bank loan. Save up as much money as you can afford and take it to the loan officer at the bank. Tell him you need to re-establish your credit and that you would like the bank to help you at no risk to them. This is how it works. Let's say, for example, you have $500. Ask for a $500 loan from the bank with the understanding that you deposit the $500 you already have into a savings account and withdraw from it only to make the loan repayments. Many banks will agree to this since they have the total amount in their control the entire time.

Once you get the loan, make double payments on it. The only cost to you will be the difference between the interest rate on the savings account and the interest rate on the loan. It will be minimal and well worth the newly-established credit. Once you have made several payments, you will be in a position to go to another bank and do the same thing again. Put the money into a savings account and pay it back ahead of time. Now you have two bank loans which were paid back early. Make sure they are recorded on your credit record. Your credit record is already in much better shape!

Using this dual strategy, you can turn your bad credit around in about six months. If you do this, and follow the rest of the advice given in this book, you will never again face the humiliation of "credit denied."

By the way, if your application for credit is ever turned down, you have a legal right to know why. Always ask in order to ensure that the potential loaner is not working from some false assumptions which can be corrected.

Co-signing

Co-signing is one form of credit rehabilitation I have not mentioned. The Bible calls it giving surety. This means one person uses his name to secure a loan for another. It is using one person's good name to cover for the bad name of another, or in some cases, covering a person who has not yet established a name for himself. Proverbs 17:18 tells us, **A man without sense gives a pledge, and becomes surety in the presence of his neighbor.** Proverbs 11:15 says, **He who gives surety for a stranger will smart for it, but he who hates suretyship is secure.**

Personally, I have known many relationships that have been ruined through entering into unwise business agreements with friends or family members. It is much better for all parties concerned that you find your own way out of a bad financial situation.

Borrowing

The Bible is full of practical stories and examples about money and material things. We can all identify with the servant in 2 Kings 6:5. He went off to fell some trees, but as he swung his axe, the head fell off and landed in deep water. The Bible records him as crying out, **Alas, my master! It was borrowed.**

Many people who borrow know the same gut-wrenching feeling of anguish that this servant must have felt. There is a place for borrowing money, but it must be done skillfully and with a purpose. The idea is to borrow only to put yourself in a lending position.

In our parents' day, if a person wanted something, they saved until they could afford to buy it. Today, we tend to charge it to our credit card and worry about "really" paying for it later. Somewhere between these two ends of the spectrum is the balance, and we need to find it.

What you borrow money for is very important. Never use credit to buy groceries or perishable items. (When I talk about credit, I am referring to the amount which is not paid off, but carried over at the end of the month.) You will be paying for the food long after it has been eaten. If you can't afford an expensive dinner out, don't go. If you can't afford meat for a week or a month, buy lentils. Promise yourself you will never use borrowed money to cover perishable items and day-to-day expenses. It is a sure way to commit financial suicide. How can you ever climb out of a hole if you are at the same time digging it deeper?

Another category of items is those things which are not perishable, but which lose their value quickly. Furniture, equipment and cars fit into this category. Buying these items with credit is better than buying food or perishables with it, but if you get into difficulties, you do not have the option of selling the item to recover the full cost of what you paid for it. The wisest use of borrowing power is to use the money only to get you ahead of the game.

For instance, last year I borrowed $30,000 to purchase a home. It wasn't a great home, but it was selling very cheap. One year later, I sold it for $60,000. I had used credit to advance my own financial plans. That is what I mean by skillfully borrowing to put yourself in a lending position. If I had spent that $30,000 on a cruise or a birthday present, I would have to pay it back painstakingly, with no extra resources to help me, and only a memory or a depreciating item to show for it. By being skillful, I now have about $28,000 of my own that I can put to work for me.

Never ever borrow money without some realistic plan of how you intend to pay it back.

Breaking Free of Debt's Paralyzing Effect

If you have been burdened with a "bad" name for some time, you may need to break a spirit of debt over your life. Often, when I counsel individuals and couples with financial problems, they are in despair. A cloud of hopelessness seems to hover over them. Recently, I saw a poster that read, "I owe so much, I can hardly pay attention." While it may be funny, there is much truth to that statement. Debt can have a paralyzing effect. You will never get out and stay out of debt until you have an optimistic view of what God can do for you in the situation you are in.

David addressed this issue in Psalm 42:11:

> **Why are you cast down, O my soul, and why are you disquieted within me? Hope in God; for I shall again praise him, my help and my God.**

It is imperative that you get hold of your emotions and have a positive mindset about the possibilities of your financial situation. Without it, you will never make any progress.

I like to think of the instance where the young boy gave Andrew the five barley loaves and the two fish to share with the multitude (John 6:1-14). Andrew's reaction was like ours would be: **What are they among so many?** (Verse 9).

How many of us see debt this way? The loaves and the fishes are what we have at our disposal, and the crowd is all those debt collectors waiting to divide it up. We have so little compared to what we need that it seems too insignificant to even consider. But look at what Jesus did. He took the five loaves and the two fish, blessed it, broke it into pieces and gave it to His disciples to distribute to the crowd. Everyone was fed!

When you have done all that you know to do, Jesus will enter the situation and show you what He can do. Jesus multiplied one little boy's lunch until it was enough to feed a multitude.

Don't fall into hopelessness over your financial situation. The same Jesus who fed the multitude from five loaves and two fish is looking out for your interests. If you have the faith to present all you have to Him, no matter how insignificant it may seem, He is able to bring you out of your impossible situation.

Throughout the Bible, we are told that Jesus Christ is our Redeemer. *Redeemer* literally means "to free by arranging or repaying." If you cooperate with God, He will redeem your situation. That is His nature, and it is His promise to us as believers.

If your good name has been tarnished, ask God how, with His help, you can redeem it. There is tremendous power in a good name.

8
Tithing

Jeff was a young family man. He felt God prompting him to give $5,000 to his church's building fund. Out of obedience to God, he paid the money to the church, even though it represented a lot of money to him and his wife. Within days, Jeff began to have second thoughts and regrets about giving the money. The fear of poverty began to eat at him.

Jeff voiced doubts about what he had done to members of the church, telling them he had made a drastic mistake in giving that amount of money. When the church elders heard about the situation, they decided to give the money back, since giving it had obviously become a stumbling block to Jeff.

Almost immediately, Jeff began to pull out of church activities. He never seemed to have enough money and began working excessive overtime. Soon he was spending more time at work than he was at home, and his marriage began to suffer. Within a year of receiving his money back, Jeff was in a bad position. He had swapped that which is eternal for that which is temporal. In the process, he had become a workaholic, and his marriage was in ruins.

Jeff allowed his circumstances to set his priorities. After obeying God and giving the money, he began to fear that he wouldn't have enough left to survive on, so he backed out of his commitment and took his money back. He needed more money, and again, he allowed his circumstances to dictate his priorities by working excessively long hours.

We are all capable of doing the same thing as Jeff. Allowing our circumstances to dictate what our priorities should be is one of the most detrimental things we can do as Christians. Our circumstances, especially if we perceive them to be grim, cloud our ability to make wise decisions. Like Jeff, we begin to falter in obeying God, especially in the area of giving. We see our situation as too desperate and can see ways we think we can "better" use the money we would have tithed.

Indeed, many well-meaning Christian leaders teach that you should pay your bills and get yourself in a position where you can afford to pay tithes. But there comes a time when you must do things because you believe they are the right things to do before God, not because they are the convenient or the comfortable thing to do. The question with giving should not be, "Can I afford to give?" but "Can I afford not to give?"

If I analyzed the times in my life where my position was financially sound enough to afford to tithe, it would amount to, at best, about 20 percent of the time. I remember so many times where I literally could not afford to tithe, but I chose to because I believed that was what God wanted me to do. At one time, my income was $2 a week. When your income is $2 a week, putting two dimes in the offering plate as your tithe becomes a big deal!

Tithing, giving one-tenth of your income to the Lord, is not something you do because you can afford to do it. It is something you do to honor God. It is an act of obedience, trust, faith and confidence in Him.

Satan would love to defeat us in the area of tithing, because he knows the wonderful freedom that comes with committing ourselves to tithing regardless of our circumstances. He would love to keep us in bondage to our circumstances, where our energies are focused on us rather than on God. But I have discovered a remedy, a way to defeat Satan, and it will work in any area of our lives, not just when dealing with tithing. That remedy is doing the opposite of what Satan wants us to do. If someone is getting

on our nerves, we should go over to them and give them
a big hug and tell them, "I love you, I appreciate you and
I am praying for you."

By responding in the opposite spirit, we negate what
Satan is trying to achieve in our lives. When my finances
are not doing well, and I feel the urge to tighten my grip
on what I have, I *give*. It works every time.

The Roots of Tithing

Before we go too far in our discussion of tithing, we
need to look at the roots of it and the reasons for it.

Tithing is first mentioned in the context of giving one-
tenth to God in the book of Leviticus.

> **All the tithe of the land, whether of the seed of
> the land or of the fruit of the trees, is the Lord's; it
> is holy to the Lord.**
>
> **And all the tithe of herds and flocks, every tenth
> animal of all that pass under the herdsman's staff, shall
> be holy to the Lord.**
>
> **Leviticus 27:30,32**

From this point on, tithing became an accepted part of
the Jews' service and devotion to God.

The last mention of tithing in the Old Testament is in
Malachi:

> **Will man rob God? Yet you are robbing me. But
> you say, "How are we robbing thee?" In your tithes
> and offerings.**
>
> **You are cursed with a curse, for you are robbing
> me; the whole nation of you.**
>
> **Bring the full tithes into the storehouse, that there
> may be food in my house; and thereby put me to the
> test, says the Lord of hosts, if I will not open the
> windows of heaven for you and pour down for you
> an overflowing blessing.**
>
> **I will rebuke the devourer for you, so that it will
> not destroy the fruits of your soil; and your vine in the
> field shall not fail to bear, says the Lord of hosts.**
>
> **Malachi 3:8-11**

The verses are explicitly clear. Unless we are paying tithes to God, we are under a curse and the influence of the devourer (Satan). On the other hand, God promises that if we will honor Him with our tithes, He will pour blessings down upon us.

> **Honor the Lord with your substance and with the first fruits of all your produce;**
>
> **Then your barns will be filled with plenty, and your vats will be bursting with wine.**
> **Proverbs 3:9,10**

God is saying that if we honor Him with first fruits, which is tithing, He will take care of our source of wealth. Honor Him, and He will honor us.

Many people say, "That was in the Old Testament. Tithing isn't really mentioned in the New Testament. There is no command that we should do it, so obviously it isn't really important today."

Certainly tithing is a very important practice in the Old Testament that is not emphasized by name in the New Testament. However, the real inference of this statement is that the Old Testament is almost superfluous, despite the fact that it takes up two-thirds of the pages in our Bible. It is there for us to pick through and take out the pieces we like, but we are under no obligation to live by it. But this is *not* what Jesus said.

In Matthew 5:18, Jesus states, **For truly, I say to you, till heaven and earth pass away, not an iota, not a dot, will pass from the law until all is accomplished.** Jesus certainly didn't believe that the law, as recorded in the Old Testament, was finished. That won't happen until heaven and earth pass away, and that hasn't happened yet.

In Luke 11:42, when Jesus was addressing the Pharisees, He said, **But woe to you Pharisees! for you tithe mint and rue and every herb, and neglect justice and the love of God; these you ought to have done, without neglecting the others.**

The strong inference in this scripture is that tithing was something they needed to do. Jesus didn't tell the Pharisees to stop tithing and give their attention to justice and the love of God. No, He told them to do these things as well as keep on tithing: ...**These you ought to have done, without neglecting the others.**

Jesus obviously considered tithing a normal part of devotion to God. He is not recorded anywhere telling people they should not tithe. While the New Testament may not refer directly to tithing, it is bursting with references on giving. *Giving* is assumed by the New Testament writers to be a normal part of the Christian's life.

Thus, by stated fact and inference from the Old and New Testaments, we know that the first 10 percent of our income is God's. And full obedience to His desire is what releases blessings into our lives from Him.

Testing the Heart

An interesting story is told in 1 Kings 17:8-16:

Then the word of the Lord came to him,

"Arise, go to Zarephath, which belongs to Sidon, and dwell there. Behold, I have commanded a widow there to feed you."

So he arose and went to Zarephath; and when he came to the gate of the city, behold, a widow was there gathering sticks; and he called to her and said, "Bring me a little water in a vessel, that I may drink."

And as she was going to bring it, he called to her and said, "Bring me a morsel of bread in your hand."

And she said, "As the Lord your God lives, I have nothing baked, only a handful of meal in a jar, and a little oil in a cruse; and now, I am gathering a couple of sticks, that I may go in and prepare it for myself and my son, that we may eat it, and die."

And Elijah said to her, "Fear not; go and do as you have said; but first make me a little cake of it and bring it to me, and afterward make for yourself and your son.

> "For thus says the Lord the God of Israel, The jar
> of meal shall not be spent, and the cruse of oil shall
> not fail, until the day that the Lord sends rain upon
> the earth."
>
> And she went and did as Elijah said; and she, and
> he, and her household ate for many days.
>
> The jar of meal was not spent, neither did the
> cruse of oil fail, according to the word of the Lord
> which he spoke by Elijah.

Perhaps you find yourself in a similar situation as this
widow. You only have a "handful," and it's not nearly
enough to meet all the needs you have. Perhaps there are
times when you feel depressed and despondent. Perhaps
you feel like going and gathering a few sticks so you can
prepare your last meal and die. Maybe you have dug
yourself into a hole, and there seems no way out this time.

Elijah knew the woman's desperate plight, but instead
of immediately relieving her burden, he added to it. The
same is true in our lives when we commit to tithing
regularly. Suddenly, we have 10 percent less than before.

Why is this? Because God is testing our character.
Faithfulness is a highly-prized quality. God wants to test
us to see if we are faithful to Him, even when our lives are
in what appears to be a pit of despair. If we do not prove
faithful to Him in the area of financial commitment, then
how is He going to trust us with the opportunities to get
wealth that He wants to release to us?

In the same way, God was testing this widow's heart
to see if she would be faithful to the word of the Lord Elijah
brought to her. In the middle of the turmoil this woman
was feeling, Elijah said to her, **Don't fear.** This is a key.
If we are going to step out and set new priorities for our
lives, we must be aware of the paralyzing effect fear and
anxiety can have on us. We must lean on the Lord and trust
Him regardless of circumstances.

Did this widow pass the test? Yes. Despite the internal
conflict she must have felt about her situation, she was
obedient to Elijah's instructions. She prepared food for

Elijah without feeding herself and her child first. And the result was not disaster, devastation, or death. Instead, her home in Zarephath was the only one with a continuous supply of oil and flour. We are told later in the passage that it remained this way for three-and-a-half years. This woman was the least able of all the people in the city to give, yet God put His finger on her and said, ''If you will trust Me with the little you have, I will multiply it beyond your wildest dreams.'' Obviously, He did!

If you are one meal away from death, why not take a chance and give it to God? Once it is in His hands, He is able to multiple it back to you.

His Law, Our Choice

Are you as zealous in your pursuit of giving your tithe to God as you are in finding all your legitimate tax deductions? What is your rationale for paying tithes? Do you tithe because you want to, or because you feel some overbearing obligation to? Are you really being totally honest about your income? Are you paying tithes on rental income and interest, for example?

These are all good questions we need to ask ourselves from time to time. We certainly need to recognize that there are consequences in the form of withheld blessings, which God Himself administers to those who choose not to honor Him with their tithe. Yet, there is a level of obedience that can be reached where tithing becomes a joy and not a legalistic burden.

9
Discipline

Statistics show that 80 percent of those families that receive a lump sum insurance payout lose all the money in one to five years, primarily through mismanagement based on poor financial advice. Had these families followed sound financial management principles, they could have secured for themselves a steady flow of financial resources.

Truth is timeless, and this statistic would not have surprised Solomon who wrote in Proverbs: **Wealth hastily gotten will dwindle, but he who gathers little by little will increase it** (Proverbs 13:11).

People often think, ''If only I had more money, I could do this or that.'' But more often than not, more money is not their answer. The answer is more discipline! Lack of discipline equals lack of money. If you have too much month left over at the end of your money, it's a sign that you need to apply some discipline to the management of your money.

''Training, especially of the mind and character, aimed at producing self-control and obedience,'' is how the dictionary defines *discipline*. It adequately defines what we are talking about as we discuss the power of discipline in building wealth. If we want to make money, we first need to train ourselves in how to properly handle it and produce the necessary self-control we need so that it won't slip through our fingers.

There are many times, I believe, when God protects us from ourselves in the area of finances. I have a $10,000 line of credit on my checking account. God knows I can handle it now. I am not tempted to rush out to buy the first thing I see. Over the years, God has taught me discipline and self-control. Had I had the same line of credit ten years ago, it would have been my undoing.

Take Control

Christians should have more self-control than non-Christians, but alas, many Christians don't seem to exercise much self-control in the area of their personal finances. They lack discipline, and as a last resort, "believe" God for a miracle to deliver them from the prison of their gross financial mismanagement.

If you are ever going to get wealth and keep it, you must take control. You must discipline yourself. You must learn to say "no;" "no" to yourself, and "no" to the members of your family.

It is He who is giving you power to *make* **wealth** (Deuteronomy 8:18, NASB) — *make*, not receive. God does not give His people the power to win the lottery, or the power to hit it big in Las Vegas, or the power to win the Publisher's Clearing House sweepstakes! No. God gives us the power to *make* wealth. *Make* means "make."

"Make" is much more difficult than "confessing" or "speaking" finances into existence. *Making* requires discipline, time and mental energy. It also requires effort, diligence, self-control and knowledge. You will not make money apart from discipline. If you are not a disciplined person, you will be poor the rest of your life. I don't mean by this that you will necessarily be on welfare. Rather, you will live with a measurable degree of lack until you die, nowhere near the level of wealth you could have reached with the application of discipline.

Have you ever noticed that certain catch verses fade in and out of popularity? Right now, one of the verses that is in vogue is, **The sinner's wealth is laid up for the righteous** (Proverbs 13:22). Christians like to quote this verse when they see a very wealthy non-Christian or when they really need money. "God, You said that the sinner's money has been put away for me. Release it in Jesus' name," they pray.

Personally, I don't have any trouble in believing that the wealth of the sinner is laid up for Christians. My question is, "How are we going to get it into our hands?" I believe it is discipline that is going to release it to us. Don't make the foolish mistake of exercising "faith" rather than discipline.

Sometimes when I teach, people come up to me afterwards with horrified looks on their faces and ask, "Pastor Blackwell, don't you believe in miracles?" Of course I believe in miracles! But there are also principles that 99.9 percent of the time work the same for the unsaved as they do for the saved. If you follow certain principles, you will reap the results.

You can be saved, filled with the Holy Spirit, sanctified, shout the victory and speak in other tongues, but if you violate these principles in any realm, you will pay the consequences. Being saved does not give you the liberty to go outside in freezing weather without adequate clothing. If you do, you will reap the consequences. The same is true with finances. If you violate principles in the economic realm, you will pay the price, regardless of your spiritual state.

There are the exceptional times when God will overrule one of these principles and work a miracle, but don't forget that they are exceptions. God will not be pigeon-holed into performing for you. Yes, it's true that Jesus walked on water, but He only did it once. The rest of the time He used a boat!

Co-heirs and Co-workers

There are two specific promises to us as Christians. One is that we are co-laborers with Christ (1 Corinthians 3:9). The other is that we are co-heirs with Christ (Romans 8:17). The one logically follows the other. If we work (co-labor), we reap the benefits (co-heirs). A co-laborer is one who works alongside another. We are called to work alongside God. God is a worker. He worked to create heaven and earth. That is why He ordained a sabbath, a day to cease from His labors. God does not honor those who sit around and wait for Him to do all the work.

God is not going to drop blessings from the sky on us as we sit watching "The Days of Our Lives." We have to cooperate with God. He gives us a part to play.

Some Christians have poor attitudes toward work. They need to deal with them. They need to thank God that He has honored them and blessed them with a job. They need to thank Him that they can work and exercise their gifts, talents, know-how, skills and abilities. When they get up in the morning, they should thank God and look forward to doing His will, and *work is God's will!* Having such an attitude will make a great difference to the day, outlook and job.

It is not God's will that we become so rich we do not need to work. Genesis 8:22 tells us, **While the earth remains,** *seedtime and harvest,* **cold and heat, summer and winter, day and night, shall not cease.** And neither will work cease. God has ordained that we work.

A Time to Save

There is no consistency to the way finances come. You can be a corporate executive one day and out of a job the next. One week you can struggle to pay your utility bills, and the next week you may inherit thousands of dollars. Sometimes there is an abundance, sometimes there isn't. The only way to stabilize your income so there is enough left over from the abundant times to carry you through the lean times is to save. Nature gives us a model to follow.

Go to the ant, O sluggard; consider her ways, and be wise.

Without having any chief, officer or ruler,

She prepares her food in summer, and gathers her sustenance in harvest.

How long will you lie there, O sluggard? When will you arise from your sleep?

A little sleep, a little slumber, a little folding of the hands to rest,

And poverty will come upon you like a vagabond, and want like an armed man.

Proverbs 6:6-11

The ant somehow has enough wisdom implanted in its tiny brain to know that in summer, when there is an abundance of resources, it had better save some of them to see it through the lean months of winter. Our brains may be substantially larger than the ant's, but many of us haven't yet learned this simple lesson. Next time you see an ant, study it. Ants work unrelentingly with precision and determination as they go about their task of storing up food. The obvious human equivalent to this is saving money.

God's people must become saving people, because the Bible tells us that money is a protection (Ecclesiastes 7:12). God blesses you with abundance to protect you against difficult times. If you will not avail yourself of His protective provision, then you cannot expect Him to override the situation. In His mercy and grace, He may choose to do so, but don't presume upon Him. It is not part of the strategy He has set in place for you. On what do I base such a bold assertion? Let's look at the life of Joseph as recorded in Genesis chapters 41-47.

God moved Joseph into a position of power in a miraculous way by giving him the interpretation to Pharaoh's dream. Pharaoh elevated Joseph from prison to becoming his right hand man.

Since the interpretation of Pharaoh's dream was that there were going to be seven years of plenty and then seven years of famine, Joseph was a very busy man for his first seven years. Genesis tells us that he personally toured Egypt, supervising the storing of excess grain. So much grain was stored that Joseph ceased measuring it because it was . . . **in great abundance, like the sand of the sea. . .it could not be measured** (Genesis 41:49). Joseph's life moved from the miraculous to the mundane. Year after year, he arranged for storage barns to be filled with corn. He resisted requests to sell the excess and had to find ways to motivate his men to keep working.

Just as God said in Pharaoh's dream, at the end of seven years, a famine occurred. But because Joseph had been diligent to follow God's Word, there was plenty in the land of Egypt. There was enough food to feed the people in the cities for seven years. There was also enough food to sell at a profit to the neighboring nations. For Joseph, the most satisfying result must undoubtedly have been that the storing of the grain also provided the circumstances for him to be reunited with his family.

In Joseph's life, we see how the rhema word of God, combined with disciplined saving, brought provision for a whole nation. God set up the circumstances for provision through the lean time, but it was Joseph's hard work that brought it about and insured there was plenty of corn for everyone during the famine.

When the seven years of famine were finally over, the people of Egypt had all been adequately fed, and much money had been accumulated through selling. Joseph was a national hero. He had also been reconciled to his family, and his family had been given permission to settle in Goshen, the best farming land in Egypt.

Joseph is widely recognized as one of the most complete types of Jesus in the Old Testament. While I do not want to glibly take something as precious as the blood shed by our Savior to redeem our souls and equate it with saving today, Jesus is interested in saving us from the heartache and frustration of not having enough. Just as Joseph saved his family from the death and destruction of the famine, Jesus also wants to reach into our situations and equip us to withstand the hardships.

How Much Should I Save?

Elizabeth was thrilled to learn she was getting a pay raise. Immediately, she began to dream of the things she would be able to do with the extra $50 a week. She could join the health club, save for a visit to see her mother and put some aside to replenish her winter wardrobe.

For the first couple of months after her pay raise, Elizabeth had noticeably more money. But as the months went by, the extra money somehow became absorbed into the everyday costs of living. Soon, there was no extra money for the health club, the trip to her mom's, or the new winter clothes. Elizabeth found herself waiting for her next pay raise to do all the extra things of which she had dreamed.

I am sure you know what happened when she received her next pay raise: the cycle repeated itself. Once again, it wasn't long before Elizabeth didn't have enough money to put any aside for the things she had dreamed of buying.

Many of us know the scenario from personal experience. We get an additional source of income and before long we're wondering how we ever got along without the extra money. It seems to be needed just to make ends meet. It is a truism that we spend up to the level of income we receive. If we receive more, then we find more ways to spend it, until we are at about the same level of debt we were before.

Very few people ever make a practice of allocating money for savings. In fact, 90 percent of all Americans live from paycheck to paycheck. They never reach that elusive plateau where they have enough money to put some away in savings. Instead, they subconsciously choose to live one or two paychecks away from the debt collector.

If you want to get off this treadmill, you must take offensive action. Defensive action will never win a game. Fortunately, the offensive action needed is simple, straightforward and easy to implement, but it will take discipline on your part to make this action a life-long habit.

What is the solution? It is simply to give 10 percent of your income to God and give 10 percent to yourself. Take the money off the top, before you spend any of it on bills and other expenses. Take your 10 percent you give to yourself and deposit it into an account that is not readily accessible to you.

After one of my seminars, a young man, Tom, talked to me. "You must be joking!" he blurted out. "First you tell me to tithe. Now you tell me to save as well. I came here because I don't have enough money to go around, not to be told more ways to spend the little I have! Don't you understand that I can't make it as it is? If I skimmed 20 percent off the top, I would only get further behind."

I could identify with the frustration Tom felt. Do any of us have enough "spare" cash to save? If you are like me, for every dollar I have, there are five ways I can think of to spend it.

I challenged Tom to think of the protection that saving would be to his family. Since he was up to his eyeballs in debt, what difference would setting aside 10 percent make to his debt load? How much more important it would be for him to develop the habit of saving than to live in a state of perpetual dread over money. Saving would give Tom a feeling of control over his situation. Before long, his weary, defeated attitude would give way to a new positive one, and in that frame of mind, he would be able to make good decisions which would steer him out of his debt permanently.

In his book, *Financial Guidance*, Dr. James McKeever, editor of "McKeever Strategy Letter," reiterates this point. "The fact is that anyone can do this if he really wants to. It might be necessary to live in a smaller house or apartment, drive a smaller or older car, or reduce your living standard in other ways. I will grant you that it may be impossible for many individuals to tithe, save 10 percent, and maintain their existing standard of living. However, unless they take corrective measures, they will always be living up against the wire, struggling to get by. My counsel to them would be to pay God first, themselves second, then adjust their standard of living to be able to live on the other 80 percent."[6]

Remember the virtuous woman in Proverbs 31? It says, **She laughs at the time to come** (Verse 25). What a wonderful picture of confidence. She knew she had contingency plans for any situation that could befall her or her family. Not even the harsh winter snow worried her, for **all her household are clothed in scarlet** (Verse 21).

Do you have that kind of confidence? Do you rest in the knowledge that you have done all you need to do to insure your family's security? Solomon was right. Money is a defense and a protection. Store away 10 percent and you, too, will laugh at the time to come.

Only Believe

How many "faith" preachers have you heard lately preaching a message of discipline, patience and cost counting? Not many, I'm sure, because too many Christians prefer to hear how they can "believe" God for whatever it is they want. They step out in "faith," hoping, wishing that somehow, magically, the resources they require will be there when they need them. They never budget or exercise any form of control over their money because they are "leaving" it in God's hands. Most crash and burn and end up bitter and trapped by their own financial mismanagement and negligence.

God doesn't call us to a life of believing Him for our finances. He has called us to a life of discipline. God is not our "sugar daddy" who gives us everything we want when we want it. He wants to partner with us in building our wealth and securing our financial future. He waits for us to do our part before He will do His. One of the things He looks for is an effort on our part to bring discipline to the way we handle our finances.

---

[6]McKeever, James. *Financial Guidance,* Omega Publications, 1989, p. 116.

10
Opportunity

I was flicking through an issue of *Reader's Digest* when I saw an article about recent immigrants to this country and how they had become financially successful.[7]

There was the story of Jim Farooquee, an immigrant from Pakistan who had established a $200-million-a-year computer business. Tuan Huynh, a penniless Vietnamese immigrant, had started a garment company that now has annual sales of over $30 million. Allan Vernon from Jamaica came to the United States by way of England. He started a restaurant business in New York, serving the fiery Jamaican-style barbecue called jerk. His restaurant now enjoys the patronage of such famous people as Bill Cosby and Patrick Ewing of the New York Knicks.

Why have these people who started with nothing become so successful? They saw an opportunity and took it. In a city burgeoning with restaurants, Allan Vernon saw an opportunity. "I saw a lack of jerk," he says. Together with his brother, they opened Vernon's Jerk Paradise in the Bronx. Now they have another restaurant in Manhattan, and their Vernon's Jerk Sauce is available in specialty food stores across the country.

Sharing on what motivated him to start this business, Jack Vernon says, "...opportunity, and the challenge that presents. If you want to hang out and depend on the government, I guess you can. But if you want to work, this

---

[7]*Reader's Digest*, December, 1990, p. 84.

is a working country.'' Jim Farooquee puts it even more succinctly, ''Success depends on your effort.''

Charles J. Givens is a man who managed to lose three separate million-dollar fortunes in his life before he learned the principles required to keep money. Yet, today he is worth over $100 million. How can a man with so many financial disasters to his name bounce back to where he is today? It is because, like these immigrants, he knows an opportunity when he sees one and was prepared to put in the needed effort to seize that opportunity.

There are many people who manage to overcome tremendous financial odds and become financially successful. Yet, by far the majority of people have no real financial handicaps to overcome. Somehow, though, they never really get ahead like those I have mentioned. Why is this? What is the missing ingredient?

The answer is contained in one word: *attitude*. The person who goes from having nothing to being wealthy has an insatiable optimism, a personal belief that he will make it. Deep inside, he sees his lack of finances as only a temporary state, one which they most surely will rise above. As a result, they actively search for a way out of their situation. They are energized to seek creative opportunities to make money.

Thus far in our discussion of the four powers of wealth-building, we have covered the power of knowledge, a good name and discipline. These three powers require mostly effort for them to work. Opportunity is different. As Christians, we need to put in the required effort to seize the opportunity, but providing the opportunities is God's job.

Unfortunately, for many Christians, they miss the opportunities God sends them because they have the wrong attitude or disposition. Instead of having faith in God's ability to get them out of the financial hole they are in, they are busy accepting that financial hole as God's will for their life. They are stuck in a negative rut and would not spot an opportunity if God dropped it on their head!

Write this quote out and put it somewhere so you can see it every day: ''There are no hopeless situations in life; there are only men who have grown hopeless about them.'' If there are situations in your life, financial or otherwise, seek God and allow Him to reignite your sense of expectancy!

The Bible has much to say about God sending us financial opportunities. Perhaps the best example is contained in the parable of the talents recorded in Matthew 25:14-30. We have a grave tendency in the church to over-spiritualize things, and the parable of the talents has not escaped this tendency. I don't know how many sermons I have heard where the talents are referred to as just that — talents — some special ability God has given us.

From there, we spiritualize the parable to mean that we must not hold back in using the ability God has given us for the furtherance of His Kingdom. Now, that could be a possible sub-meaning to the parable, but it is not the primary meaning. The word *talent* does not mean a special God-given ability. Rather, it is a money term like *dollar*, used to convey a certain unit of currency. In Jesus' times, it was measured in terms of talents of silver or gold. In today's terms, it would be worth about $30,000. So in this parable, Jesus is talking about a master handing out money to his servants.

> **For it will be as when a man going on a journey called his servants and entrusted to them his property;**
>
> **To one he gave five talents, to another two, to another one, to each according to his ability. Then he went away.**
>
> **He who had received the five talents went at once and traded with them; and he made five talents more.**
>
> **So also, he who had the two talents made two talents more.**
>
> **Matthew 25:14-17**

These two men took their money and immediately went out to negotiate. They did not procrastinate. Each one had already worked out how they would invest their money, and when they received it, they went out and immediately put their plan into action. Both of them quickly made a 100 percent profit.

> **But he who had received the one talent went and dug in the ground and hid his master's money.**
>
> **Matthew 25:18**

This man took the money entrusted to him and buried it. The money was in the ground. It's the same with us. If the money God has entrusted to us is not increasing, if we aren't seeing any profit from it, then it is as good as being in the ground. Many things grow in the ground, but money isn't one of them! When you put money in the ground, it is buried. It isn't making any profit.

> **Now after a long time the master of those servants came and settled accounts with them.**
>
> **And he who had received the five talents came forward, bringing five talents more, saying, "Master, you delivered to me five talents; here I have made five talents more."**
>
> **His master said to him, "Well done, good and faithful servant; you have been faithful over little, I will set you over much; enter into the joy of your master."**
>
> **And he also who had the two talents came forward, saying, "Master, you delivered to me two talents; here I have made two talents more."**
>
> **His master said to him, "Well done, good and faithful servant; you have been faithful over little, I will set you over much; enter into the joy of your master."**
>
> **Matthew 25:19-23**

Notice that the word *joy* is used in this passage. There is a natural joy that comes with any type of productive activity, be it planting a garden, birthing a baby, or making a wise investment that yields a good return. We receive joy from seeing the increase produced. Conversely, when we see things being squandered, and when we don't take advantage of opportunities that come our way, there is a natural sadness and regret. It is a reflex mechanism God has placed within us.

It also brings great joy to God when He lays an opportunity at our feet, and we pick it up and cause it to increase.

> **He also who had received the one talent came forward, saying, "Master, I knew you to be a hard man, reaping where you did not sow, and gathering where you did not winnow;**
>
> **"So I was afraid and I went and hid your talent in the ground. Here you have what is yours."**
>
> **But his master answered him, "You wicked and slothful servant! You knew that I reap where I have not sowed, and gather where I have not winnowed?**
>
> **"Then you ought to have invested my money with the bankers, and at my coming I should have received what was my own with interest."**
>
> **Matthew 25:24-27**

I find it very interesting that Jesus' words in this scripture passage about finances are just as relevant today as they were then. The very least you could do with your money then was put it in the bank to draw interest, and that is still true today. You are not maximizing your money by putting it in the bank, but at least you are doing something with it. Interest rates on bank savings accounts are around 5.5 percent. However, there are mutual funds available that pay 20 percent or more interest on your money, much more than you could ever get at a bank.

Why did this servant bury his money instead of investing it? Basically, because of fear. He was afraid of his master's reaction to him if he invested it and somehow lost the money in the process. So he took the safest route he knew: he buried the money.

I meet Christians like this. They won't take any type of risks with what God has given them because they are afraid of losing it. Instead, they take what God has given them and hide it or bury it. They fail to see that God is more severe in His judgment of those people who do nothing with what He gives them than He is of those who try and fail.

> **So take the talent from him, and give it to him who has the ten talents.**
>
> **For to every one who has will more be given, and he will have abundance; but from him who has not, even what he has will be taken away.**
>
> **Matthew 25:28,29**

Notice, *it is maximizing what you have that qualifies you for more.* If you take the $100 God blesses you with and have the attitude, ''What's a $100? I can't do anything with it,'' you will lose it. If, on the other hand, you do the right thing with it and see it grow and produce, then God will entrust you with more. Maximize what you have, and you will be given more.

What was the consequence to this servant as a result of his lack of initiative?

> **And cast the worthless servant into the outer darkness; there men will weep and gnash their teeth.**
>
> **Matthew 25:30**

This man was consigned to hell for burying money! It was obviously a serious shortcoming from Jesus' point of view. The man's actions were considered sin and were punishable by hell. Many people live each day in the hell of a punishing lifestyle simply because they have taken what God has given them and buried it rather than make it earn a return.

There is inequity in the parable. The man who had the single talent didn't have as much as the other two servants. However, he had the same opportunity to do something with what he had. If he had taken that opportunity and multiplied his money as the other two had, he would have received his portion, just as the other two received theirs.

We may not all receive the same amount from God, but we all have the same opportunity to do something with it. That's what counts. God has given each of us the power to increase what we have. Somehow, though, in the Christian church, we have managed to relegate money-making to something offensive and worldly. Our highest ideal for people when they become Christians is that they become a preacher and live by "faith," which some people believe involves quitting their good "secular" job and leaving their income behind. But this attitude is both unbiblical and unproductive.

If God has given you the gift of making money, then *make money.* The highest calling you can have is using the gifts and abilities God has given you to their fullest potential. Today, the church needs men and women who are called and ordained to finance the vision of the Kingdom of God, not more preachers living by faith.

It is reassuring to know that there are people in my congregation who know they are called to finance God's Kingdom work. I remember when the church eldership decided we needed a larger parking lot. I mentioned it once to the congregation, and a member came to me with a check for multi-thousands of dollars. I can preach, but I can't preach a parking lot into existence. It takes money. Remember, the writer of Ecclesiastes says money answers all things. We needed a thing, and God gave someone the ability to provide it. If we all work together in this way, God will be glorified.

Many years ago, before I learned these principles, our church offerings were often like an auction. "Who can give another $8?" "Who's got 25 cents to bring this offering up to $30?" God has a better way of doing things. If He has called you to be a part of providing material things to progress the Kingdom of God, then embrace that calling. Do it with your whole heart in a way that brings honor to Him.

The God of Opportunities

How does God bring opportunities? The first thing to understand in answering this question is that God is the most creative being in the universe. He has created opportunities for you, more imaginative and diverse than you are capable of comprehending. If you ask Him, He will open your eyes to these opportunities. Ask Him to show you the opportunity He has for dealing with your specific financial situation. Ask in faith, and believe He loves you and that He will answer your prayer.

Often, people will find that this opportunity is something already within their grasp. Moses discovered this in a dramatic way. God told Moses that He was going to lead the children of Israel out of captivity in Egypt (Exodus 4:1,2). Moses had a lot of questions about his ability to perform such a task, and said to the Lord:

> . . . **They will not believe me or listen to my voice, for they will say, "The Lord did not appear to you."**
>
> **The Lord said to him, "What is that in your hand?" He said, "A rod."**

The Lord told Moses to throw his rod on the ground, and when he did, it became a serpent. Then he picked it up, and it became a rod again. That rod became the symbol of God's power and authority that rested with Moses. It was a simple, common thing, used every day without a second thought. But God used it in bringing the children of Israel out from Egypt.

I believe the opportunity that will get you out of your Egypt, out of your financial bondage, is in your hand, within your grasp. Through utilizing it and using it wisely, you will once and for all be able to free yourself from the enslavement of being in debt to others.

Creative opportunities originate with God, and usually they are simple things. One of the opportunities God provided me as a source of income was certainly like this. I have a degree in music and love to play music and lead worship in our church, but I travel a lot. It was pointed out to me that the church did not do so well in the area of music and worship when I was away. I asked God how I could solve the problem, and the idea of taping the sound tracks of the songs onto separate tapes dropped into my mind. By doing this, the worship leader, along with our sound people, could flick the tapes in and out of the cassette deck and retain control over the flow of them, in much the same way he would if he were directing live musicians.

The idea worked very well. Within six months, I had a stack of 5,000 orders on my desk for copies of the tape tracks. People had heard about it by word of mouth. Today, "Amplified Productions," as I named it, is a thriving business. Over a period of time, we refined the concept so that one side of the tape has the words sung on it, while the other side remains just the instrumental, and we enclose a word sheet.

"Amplified Productions" is now nationwide. In fact, recently, I considered an offer by a RCA representative to distribute Amplified worship sound tracks.

The whole operation now takes me less than half an hour a week to administer. I am reaping the financial benefits of an idea God gave me. It took some initial effort on my part to get it going, but it has paid off.

What's in your hand? What creative opportunity is God waiting to birth in you? Perhaps you have a hobby you can use to make money. A hobby is something we love to do, but for which we don't get paid. Why not turn your hobby into a money-making venture? God has the ability to take whatever it is that's in your hand and work a miracle with it.

So many people minimize their talents. When it is suggested to them that they could use those talents as an avenue for creating wealth, they say, "So I love to cook. What use is that? It's no big deal." You would be amazed by the number of people and businesses who want to employ someone who can cook. Recently, I heard of two ladies who began baking cookies and taking them around to the various offices in their area. Who can resist a brownie at coffee break? They made $100 on their first day. That adds up to $2,000 a month, and it didn't even take up all their time, not to mention the fact that they were able to work from their own homes. You, too, can do similar things with your talents or hobbies, regardless of how insignificant you may think they are.

A business is basically built on finding something that a lot of people either don't want to do, or do not have the time or capability to do, and having them pay you to do that thing for them.

After giving my seminar on "Power To Get Wealth," a lady from my congregation came to see me. Thelma was in her early thirties and spent most of her time at home caring for her young children. She was looking for a way to earn some extra income for the family. We talked a little about what the thing might be that God had placed in her hand, but nothing seemed very promising. As we talked, I remembered that my wife had once commented to me how Thelma's clothes were always so impeccably ironed. I asked her if she liked to iron. "Oh, that," she replied. "Yes, I've always been good at ironing. I like to do a good job."

As we explored this possibility further, we found that it would be an ideal way for Thelma to earn some extra income, without having to leave her home. Neither would it require any extra equipment or outlay. Together, we did some calculations. With a few regular customers, she could easily earn $120 a week. That came out to $6,240 a year. If Thelma were to keep it up for thirty years, she would have earned $197,200. Remember, if you invest your money at 15 percent, the amount invested will double every five years. So I encouraged Thelma to invest what she earned and allow it to grow and produce for her. If she did this, she could "retire" from her part-time ironing career with a very large balance in the bank. Her eyes got wider and wider as we talked.

Thelma had been waiting for something "big" to happen. Instead, something that seemed almost trivial to her at first, had the potential to make a large amount of money.

I get tired of hearing people say, "I can't do much." Don't minimize what is in your hand. Having a high-paying job does not always get you ahead. Rather, it is recognizing what is in your hand and handling it wisely.

Everybody can do something. It's the enemy of our souls who tells us that we have no ability, talent, or skill. That is a lie and an indictment against God. How could God create you, yet leave no trace of Himself and His wonderful creativity in your life? He does not do that. He has given you a reservoir of talents and abilities upon which He wants you to draw. Don't make the mistake of thinking you can do nothing because your abilities are few. Instead, start with what you have, and allow God to multiply it!

Inside Information

There was once a man who had a word of prophecy. He felt God had told him that the price of certain commodities was going to decrease drastically overnight. He delivered the message to the assistant of a very powerful man in his area. The assistant mocked him: "Even if God Himself took charge of this situation, it would be impossible." So the man who had the prophecy turned to him and said, "You'll get to see what I have said come true, but it will do you no good."

True to the prophecy, a trail of very strange events led to a huge drop in the price of the commodities. The assistant lived long enough to see the dramatic drop with his own eyes, but not long enough to enjoy any bargains. He was trampled to death by the crowd that was rushing to buy the commodities.

This story is found in 2 Kings 7. The man with the prophecy was Elisha, the powerful man was the King and his assistant was the captain of the guard. And, of course, the commodities were fine meal and barley.

Imagine the ramifications if we knew what the stock market would do tomorrow, if we knew what stocks were going to rise and which ones that were going to fall. What if we knew where a major highway was going to be built, or what real estate was going to become prime land in the next five years. Imagine the difference it would make to our decisions. Well, God is quite capable of imparting this kind of knowledge to us.

Pastor John Gimenez has made multiple millions of dollars for the Kingdom of God this way. He buys the properties which God directs him to buy. Invariably, he finds that within a year the properties he was led to buy have at least doubled in value. Then he sells the property and buys another one as God directs. God has been directing him in this way for years now, and the church has benefitted tremendously as a result.

We are comfortable calling upon God for His help when choosing a marriage partner, or deciding which church we should attend, or for help in a time of need. Somehow, we stop there. However, God is interested in all aspects of our life, in leading us into all truth in every area, including finances. Ask Him for wisdom and help in how, where and when to invest your money. I constantly ask God's help in being a wise investor. In one case, an investment I felt led to make paid off 400 percent within nine months. I was glad I had taken the time to seek God's help.

Investing is a wonderful opportunity for building wealth. With some knowledge, savvy and a clear strategy, you can consistently earn very high interest on your investment. Many people confess to me their fear about investing. They are unsure of how the system works and believe there is a high amount of risk involved, but this is not the case. The system is not as complicated as we may at first think, and the risk factor is low.

I have included a section on investments so you can familiarize yourself with some of the basic information you will need in utilizing the wealth-building potential of this opportunity.

Investments: A Personal Strategy

Jack Wilson had been a company manager and a shrewd investor until his death in 1969. As a result, he left his wife, Alice, with a good sum of money. Alice Wilson, on the other hand, had never really understood much about stocks and bonds. The money was initially a worry to her, until she decided to leave it exactly where her husband had put it.

Now, over twenty years later, Alice Wilson still has not changed a thing. When her children ask her where she has invested the money, she says, "Exactly what your father chose. He knew what he was doing." Each year, one of the companies in which she has significant stock, throws a Christmas party and invites her to come. They also have flowers waiting for her when she arrives. Why not? Alice Wilson is one of their biggest investors. Were she to invest elsewhere, she could be earning at least triple the interest that this company pays.

Alice's age undoubtedly contributed to her stubbornness, but she had also made the obvious mistake of believing she had a "secure, long-term investment." Unfortunately, there is no such thing. Different investments are appropriate in different economic climates. If we do not understand how to make informed investment decisions, we will end up either sitting on investments when their comparative value has long since diminished or diversifying in an attempt to "hedge" that our good and bad investments cancel out each other.

Of all the areas in financial management, investment is perceived as the most mysterious and unpredictable. Yet, with some basic knowledge and common sense, you can safely earn at least 20 percent interest a year.

There are three main types of investments: stocks, bonds and money market funds. All three are handled by mutual funds. Mutual funds group together a combination of at least 100 stocks, bonds and money market investments. When you invest in a mutual fund, you can buy a portion of any one of the stocks, bonds, or money market investments, or any combination of the three. Because of this, your investment is much safer than if you were to individually select single stocks or bonds. It is also easy to evaluate the state of mutual funds, the closing price and Net Asset Value (NAV), which can be found in the daily newspaper.

The first step in sound investing is to always use a mutual fund. Never buy stocks or bonds individually.

There are three types of mutual funds: no-load, low-load and high-load. The term *load* refers to a sales commission, with no-load funds having no commission and high-load funds having a 4 to 9 percent commission. *All* mutual funds charge a 1 percent fee, independent of the sales commission. This 1 percent fee pays for the cost of administering no-load accounts.

Mutual fund accounts are further subdivided into front-end loads and back-end loads, depending on whether you pay the commission when you buy or sell.

In any given economy, there is only one right investment. The challenge is to identify it and invest in it until such time as the economy changes. At that time, another type of investment emerges as the best. How do you tell which is the best investment? First, you need to know a little about the economy. This is not as complex as it might seem.

You need to know the Prime Interest Rate (PIR). Once again, it can be found in the daily newspaper. The PIR moves slowly and is the main reason for the raising or lowering of stocks, bonds and money market accounts. You need to know two things about the PIR: Is it high or low? And is it moving up or down? You also need to know what the Investor's Decision Line is. Currently, it is around 9.5 percent, and it moves very slowly and infrequently.

Once you have ascertained these three things, you simply choose the correct investment for their movement, as follows. When the PIR is above the Investor's Decision Line, but falling, invest in bond funds. When it is above the Investor's Decision Line and rising, invest in money market funds. Whenever it is below the Investor's Decision Line, invest in stock funds.

It is as simple as that. Summarized below are the main points you need to know:

• Always use no-load accounts.

• Use a mutual fund to ensure you do not fall prey to individual quirks of the stock and bond markets.

• Know which way the interest rates are going and what the Investor's Decision Rate is in order to choose the correct category for the economy.

These strategies will yield at least a 20 percent return, often more. That level of interest adds up to rapid and safe wealth-building. Find out the relevant facts and try it for yourself. I promise, you will never "park" your money in a bank account again.

On a Fixed Income

People often describe themselves as being "on a fixed income." My question to them always is, "Who fixed your income?" It certainly wasn't God. In Him, the possibilities for income are unlimited, not fixed. Be careful not to categorize yourself as on a fixed income. The opportunities are there. However, we must be diligent and tenacious in our pursuit of those opportunities.

My son, Lucien, is a typical teenager. When I tell him to go and look for something, he comes back about five seconds later to tell me he has searched everywhere and can't find it. We are often like this. How long are we prepared to look before we "throw in the towel" in our search for God's opportunities? Look, and keep looking until you find what it is you seek.

I once read a quote which has often spurred me into action: "Many of life's failures are men who did not realize how close they were to success when they gave up."

What opportunities does God have for you? How close are you to realizing them? What has God put in your hand that could transform your circumstances? You will never know the answer to these questions unless you diligently search for them. And if you search for them with your whole heart, you will not be disappointed. God is faithful!

11

Families and Money

Perhaps no other single thing puts so much tension and stress on a family as finances. Financial pressure is like acid rain, eating away slowly at the fabric of the family. But, as I have pointed out in this book, we don't have to settle for this situation. We can make changes that will once and for all deal with the problem.

There are several practical steps we can take regarding families and money. The first is to assess the financial decision-making process in the family and establish who is best qualified to make the decisions. Second, we need to start training our children in how to handle money. Last, we must make adequate provision for our family in case of our early or untimely death.

Who Makes the Decisions?

Most of us, when we look back at who made the financial decisions in our family, recognize that our father made most, if not all, of them. Singlehandedly, he carried the weight of the family's financial situation. But is this right? Do men have some inalienable right to make all the financial decisions in the family? Should they be the only ones to shoulder the financial burden?

I don't think it was ever intended that men should bear all the financial weight in a marriage. Marriage is a partnership, and scripture tells us, **the two shall become one.** Thus, no one partner has the right to make all the major financial decisions. Financial decisions in a marriage first need to be discussed, and then together, a course of action needs to be determined.

Behold, how good and pleasant it is when brothers *(and husbands and wives)* **dwell in unity!** writes David in Psalm 133:1. How true this is. If a couple will talk about the financial decisions before them and come to a mutual decision about what to do, joy and harmony will replace the acid rain of tension and strife.

Making financial decisions is one thing. Implementing them is quite another. I believe the partner in the marriage who has the most interest, expertise, or time to carry the decisions through should be the one who does the implementing. This may not be the man. Men need to lay aside their egos and let their wives do the job if they have a better understanding, or are better qualified to do it. If you are in any doubt about the Biblical validity of women handling money, read the list below of some of the attributes of a virtuous woman as found in Proverbs 31:

• The heart of her husband trusts in her, and he will have no lack of gain (Verse 11).

• She seeks wool and flax, and works with willing hands (Verse 13).

• She considers a field and buys it; with the fruit of her hands she plants a vineyard (Verse 16).

• She perceives that her merchandise is profitable (Verse 18).

• She opens her hand to the poor, and reaches out her hands to the needy (Verse 20).

• She is not afraid of snow for her household, for all her household are clothed in scarlet (Verse 21).

• She makes linen garments and sells them; she delivers girdles to the merchant (Verse 24).

• She looks well to the ways of her household, and does not eat the bread of idleness (Verse 27).

All of these things have to do with finances. The virtuous woman buys and trades, sells and plans ahead.

She reaches out to the needy and has won her husband's complete trust. Many women are entirely capable of running the family finances. In fact, they are often more capable than their husbands.

Training Children

As Christian parents, we all acknowledge that we have an obligation to train our children. All of us, I'm sure, can quote Proverbs 22:6 from memory:

> **Train up a child in the way he should go, and when he is old he will not depart from it.**

We diligently try to walk this verse out each day with our children and train them in developing their spiritual life, character, intellectual capacities, social graces and a myriad of other things that a child must learn on his way to adulthood. But do we take this obligation seriously when it comes to teaching our children how to handle finances?

Regardless of the lifestyle our children choose, they will encounter financial decisions along the way. If they are unaware of how to make good financial choices, money may well destroy them. The financial decisions and choices we face today are far more complex than those our parents faced, and our children will face even more complex decisions and choices. If we neglect to train them in how to go about making these decisions, we do them a grave disservice. Most rich people take this responsibility seriously. They teach their children the financial "ropes" in order to keep the money in the family. How much more should we do this for the Kingdom of God?

To effectively train a child, we must use a combination of Word and action, theory and practice. Children must know the reasons behind what we do before they ever emulate it. Every Saturday morning, our family has devotions together. Lois and I take this opportunity to teach the theory of Christian living. Over the years, tithing, good stewardship and the advantages of a good education have come up many times. We share our convictions with the children on these matters, and show them scriptures which affirm what we believe and practice. This has helped them greatly over the years. Not only do they see what we do, but they know why we do it.

Parents who are secretive about their finances are not providing an adequate role model for their children. It is not a sign of weakness if your children know the truth about the family finances. Indeed, they will be much more sympathetic towards having to wait for the things they want if they understand their needs in the wider context of the family's financial resources. Money doesn't grow on trees, and children need to know that, as well as where it comes from, where it goes and how to handle it in between.

Even very young children need the consequences of good financial choices demonstrated to them. Last summer, Janet and her two daughters, ages four and seven, were staying at an expensive hotel in Orlando, Florida. The girls wanted to go swimming in one of the hotel pools, and as they were getting ready, Janet realized she had left the sunscreen at home. She found her purse and headed for the small poolside shop.

To her dismay, the lotion was twice the price it normally is in a convenience store. She explained to the girls how expensive the sunscreen was and asked if they would mind walking a quarter mile down the street with her to a convenience store where they could buy it at a better price. They agreed, and off they went.

When they got to the store, the sunscreen was half the price it was at the hotel. Janet pointed out to the girls that they had saved $4 just by taking a short walk. To reinforce the idea, she allowed them to spend the $4 they had saved. Each girl walked proudly back to the hotel with their new Barbie coloring books tucked under their arms, a tangible reminder of the need to shop around for the best price before you buy.

It is also good to try to bring many of the aspects of the family finances into a family team context. Let's say, for example, your monthly electric bill is too high. Bring the family together. Look at the problem, and talk about some solutions that will help reduce the bill. Maybe you could make a deal with your children. Monitor the next three electric bills, and agree to pay them the amount of money they save on the bill by reducing their power consumption. You've lost nothing. You would have had to pay out that amount anyway if your children hadn't reduced their electrical usage. In the meantime, your children have gained an awareness of the relationship between switching off appliances and saving money. At the end of the agreed three months, the children will have established new habits which could well reduce your electric bill for quite some time.

With children, you must be very specific about your financial expectations. Get into the habit of laying out parameters for them. If your teenager makes a lot of long distance telephone calls, say to them: "I will pay for the first five minutes of the call. After that, it is your responsibility. Here is a timer. Write down how long you talk. The rate is 40 cents a minute." Record the details of the agreements you make with your children so you can hold them accountable. Remember, God never left anything to memory. He always recorded the details.

If, for instance, you agree to spend $250 on "back-to-school" clothes for your teenage daughter, put it down in writing. Together, keep records of how much you spend on clothes, and when the figure gets to $250, there will be no room for misunderstanding. It will be recorded in black and white.

Many times parents allow situations to develop, and then become angry about them when it is too late to do anything constructive about them. Such action only puts a strain on everyone. Give your children very clear guidelines ahead of time. By doing so, you will have a lot less financial stress in your family.

Often, the early years of marriage are years of financial hardship. Children come and strain the already-tight budget, and everyone ends up making sacrifices. When things become more financially stable and secure, we must remember to share the good times with our children. Paul said in Romans 8:17:

> **...We suffer with him in order that we may also be glorified with him.**

My four children have endured some very lean times in our family, so my wife and I make sure that when God blesses us, we pass that blessing on to them.

In 1990, I took my fourteen-year-old son, Lucien, to Miami to see the Notre Dame Fighting Irish and the Colorado Buffaloes play in the Orange Bowl. I booked a beautiful suite in a hotel, and we flew first class. I wanted to expose Lucien to the very best. Some might look upon this as a waste of money. I look at it as an investment in my son. We had a wonderful time together enjoying God's blessing.

While we were there, I was also able to share with him why we had this blessing to enjoy. I sat him down and said, "Lucien, do you know why you are here? Do you know how you got here, while all those other students are back in school struggling through their classes? You are here because of the blessings of God. The reason we are living like this is because of the goodness of God. If you want to maintain this kind of lifestyle, then you better do what your daddy is doing. That is being obedient to God, living a holy life and doing the will of God, whatever it may be. All that we have, the house we live in and the cars we drive, everything we do and have is because of God's grace in our lives. Because I have proven myself faithful, He has blessed me. Now you are the recipient of that blessing. The day will come when you will be the man of your own house. If you are going to maintain this kind of lifestyle, you will have to do it through being faithful to God."

During a summer break, we took our four children to Disney World. We rented an executive home nearby and had a week of lavish luxury. In that environment, we had some wonderful conversations with our children. We explained to them how God had given us the power to make the money we were spending, and we challenged them that if they wanted to enjoy the financial blessings of God, then they needed to follow the guidelines we had taught them.

It would be an indictment on me as a father if my children had to read this book to find out about finances. By the time they have lived with me for twenty years, they should know all that is contained in this book and more. If they do not, then I have failed in imparting the truths God has taught me to the next generation. We are mandated to pass on to our children our understanding of God. We see this in Jewish culture where so much is centered around conveying how and why God had shown them favor at various times. We, too, must make a conscious effort to pass on to our children what the Lord has taught us.

And these words which I command you this day shall be upon your heart;

And you shall teach them diligently to your children, and shall talk of them when you sit in your house, and when you walk by the way, and when you lie down, and when you rise.

And you shall bind them as a sign upon your hand, and they shall be as frontlets between your eyes.
Deuteronomy 6:6-8

Ultimately, children learn best when faced with real-life situations that require them to make choices. That is why I think it is a mistake to give a child an allowance beyond the age of thirteen. What are we trying to teach them? That the world is going to pay them for breathing? That regardless of the effort they put into life, there will always be a check waiting for them at the end of the week? A lot of children need a good dose of reality therapy: *when you put in the work, you reap the rewards.* That's what life is really like.

Our girls, Stacy and Alana, had to take summer jobs to help put themselves through college. I could easily have paid their whole way and left them to relax all summer long. But what message would I be sending them? I firmly believe if a person does not have to work for something, they will never respect it. Don't rob your children of that satisfaction.

Recently, I read an inspiring article about an 18-year-old black girl from Georgia. Her father died when she was twelve, leaving her mother to struggle to support three children.

Angel Ragins relays in the article how her parents began to teach her self-reliance at an early age. They did not give her money but gave her ways to earn it. By the time she was in seventh grade, she knew she wanted to go to college and that she would have to find a way to finance it herself. In twelfth grade, she would come home from her after-school job at 11:30 p.m. and begin filling in applications for scholarships. She completed over 200 of them, and the results were astounding. She won scholarships to over thirty colleges, valued at over $315,000, setting what officials believe to be a state record.

"We often see students with Angel's talent," says Georgann Reaves, the faculty adviser to the high school's literary magazine. "We don't often see students with Angel's determination and willingness to work on her own to get what she wants."

Angel gives hints to other high schoolers who want to do the same. Among them are: maintain a good reputation, research the things you are interested in, keep good records and work hard.[8]

As I read the article, I smiled to myself. Angel had stumbled upon the power to get wealth. She may not have started life with many so-called "advantages," but she did have parents who trained her in the areas of discipline,

---

[8]*Parade Magazine*. Sunday, September 15, 1991, p. 4.

knowledge and the power of a good name. I would like to
know where she ends up ten years from now.

Where will your children be ten years from now? Still
relying on you for a handout? Still waiting for you to
organize things for them? You need to actively prepare your
children to become financially mature. There is no better
time to start training them than *today*. If you have neglected
this area of your family life, it would be beneficial to read
Parenting With Love and Logic, Teaching Children Responsibility
by Foster Cline, M.D. and Jim Fay (Navpress, 1990). This
book offers some excellent and practical advice on these
issues.

A Time to Die

> In those days Hezekiah became sick and was at
> the point of death. And Isaiah the prophet the son of
> Amoz came to him, and said to him, "Thus says the
> Lord: Set your house in order; for you shall die, you
> shall not recover."
>
> Then Hezekiah turned his face to the wall, and
> prayed to the Lord.
>
> Then the word of the Lord came to Isaiah:
>
> "Go and say to Hezekiah, Thus says the Lord, the
> God of David your father: I have heard your prayer,
> I have seen your tears; behold, I will add fifteen years
> to your life."
>
> Isaiah 38:1,2,4,5

Whenever I read through this passage about Hezekiah,
I am struck by how God, through the prophet Isaiah, told
Hezekiah not only that he was about to die, but that he also
needed to get his affairs in order so that his family wouldn't
face a huge, tangled mess after his death.

After Hezekiah sought God, the time frame for his
death was extended another fifteen years. Could he have
needed that much time to get his affairs in order?

The Bible also makes reference to another man who
died, only this man received no prior warning from God.

We pick up his story after his death. His widow comes running to see Elisha, the prophet.

> **Your servant my husband is dead; and you know that your servant feared the Lord, but the creditor has come to take my two children to be his slaves.**
> **2 Kings 4:1**

The man is to be commended because of his spiritual astuteness in the things of God. He recognized Elisha as a man of God and served him faithfully. In the spiritual realm, he seemed to have it all together. But what about the material realm? Things weren't so good in the material realm, for he had made no provision for an untimely death. As a result, his whole family was in turmoil. Not only did they have to bear the grief of his death, but his wife faced the prospect of spending the rest of her life alone, no sons to support her. They would be forced to become slaves as a result of their father's financial failings.

We hear the pathos in this woman's dilemma: **Your servant feared the Lord, but the creditor has come.** Putting it in today's vernacular, we might say, "He was a godly, Christian man. He left the children a wonderful spiritual heritage, but since his death, the children have had to go into foster homes, and his wife is working as a live-in housemaid in a cheap hotel." Quite a problem! A giant in the spiritual realm, but a disaster in the material realm.

One Sunday, as I was preparing to preach a sermon on this passage, I became curious as to how old the man might have been when he died. I decided to ask the Lord, since He was there when it happened. To my surprise, I got a very clear answer back from God. "You want to know how old the man was when he died? He was old enough to die." Old enough to die. We're all old enough to die today, tomorrow, next month. Therefore, we all need to make arrangements now, so that those we leave behind won't have to sort through a tangled mess of disorganized affairs.

A Tale of Two Widows

Susan, a vivacious woman in her late forties, has a good job in a large accounting firm, a son studying art in Paris and an infectious confidence and joy about life. Several years earlier, her husband, Chad, contracted a rare muscle disease that caused his body to slowly shut down.

When the disease was finally diagnosed, the prognosis wasn't good. Chad had a year to live at best. He rose to the occasion and began to prepare his wife for life without him. He had always handled the finances, and Susan knew little about their financial situation, other than that there was always plenty of money. Chad knew there was enough money in investments to keep Susan and their son comfortable for the rest of their lives, if she handled it wisely. He found a good community college that offered a course of study in basic accounting and urged Susan to enroll in it.

Although in great pain, he took many hours to go over the family finances with her, giving her advice and quizzing her on how she would face certain situations. By the time Chad died eleven months later, Susan had completed one year of college and had a good understanding of their financial situation.

Most widows face a steady decline in their assets from the time of their husband's death, but Susan is an exception. She went on and attained an accounting degree and an ever-increasing confidence in financial matters.

Joan found herself in an entirely different situation. Her husband, Jim, developed an inoperable brain tumor. Twenty days after it was discovered, Jim was dead. During that time, he had tried to concentrate on being healed and refused to "give Satan a foothold" by discussing the possibility of his death with anyone. When he died, he left no life insurance and a new mortgage on their first home.

Joan was now a widow with three small children. Her father-in-law tried his best to help her, but she was too distraught and incompetent to make wise financial decisions. Within a year, she lost the house and was living back home with her parents. This was a very unsatisfactory arrangement, so with few options available to her, she rushed into a second marriage. This proved to be a disaster, and she divorced five years later.

I would like to tell you that Susan and Chad were Christians, and Jim and Joan were not. Unfortunately, it was the other way around.

If we truly love our families, we must make sure they are properly cared for after we are gone. Think of Jesus' last days on earth. He prepared those He was leaving behind in many ways. He prepared Peter for the emotional turmoil he would face. He promised the disciples He would send a Comforter when He had gone, and He even looked down from the cross to entrust His mother into John's keeping. Jesus was a man who was prepared for His death, and He prepared those around Him for it, too. Are we as prepared for death?

I have relatives who refuse to write wills because they have a fear of dying. They reason that if they don't have a will, they can't die yet. That's ludicrous. Not having a will won't lengthen their lives. It will just show everyone how stupid and lacking in common sense they were. Make sure you have a will. Buy some term life insurance to protect your assets. Protect yourself and your family.

If you need more specific information, I would heartily recommend the book, *Leave Your House in Order* by John Watts (published by Tyndale). It offers a comprehensive coverage of this topic.

As a pastor, I have seen too many sad situations to believe that being a Christian immunizes a family from heartache. You don't want your family to have to endure the pain of lack, want, poverty and need after you are gone, simply because you didn't plan ahead. Make sure that your partner has a good understanding of the family's financial situation. Keep your records in a system that someone else can follow. I repeat, get some term life insurance to protect your assets and make a will. Do not allow it to be said of you, ''Your servant feared the Lord, but the creditors have come.''

12

Wisdom and Warning

I built houses and planted vineyards for myself;

I made myself gardens and parks, and planted in them all kinds of fruit trees.

I made myself pools from which to water the forest of growing trees.

I bought male and female slaves, and had slaves who were born in my house; I had also great possessions of herds and flocks, more than any who had been before me in Jerusalem.

I also gathered for myself silver and gold and the treasure of kings and provinces.

Ecclesiastes 2:4-8

This is Solomon's inventory. God allowed him to experience unprecedented wealth. He became vastly more wealthy than any of his predecessors. Unfortunately, Solomon's earthly wealth nearly choked out his relationship with God. There are some scholars who question whether Solomon was following God at the time of his death. I believe he was. As I read the latter half of Proverbs and the Book of Ecclesiastes, I see the heart of a repentant man.

Two things I ask of thee; deny them not to me before I die:

Remove far from me falsehood and lying; give me neither poverty nor riches; feed me with the food that is needful for me.

> Lest I be full, and deny thee, and say, "Who is
> the Lord?" or lest I be poor, and steal, and profane the
> name of my God.
>
> **Proverbs 30:7-9**

So much of Solomon's energy had been poured into accumulating wealth that he had lost sight of the single most important thing in his life: his relationship with the Lord. Finally, though, he realized the error of his way and humbly asked God to give him what he needed, no more, no less.

Get Rich Quick

Tens of thousands of dollars change hands each day in a futile attempt to get rich quick. The desire for riches is a snare that has destroyed countless families and individuals. It can manifest itself in many ways from selfishness to gambling to embezzling. If left unchecked, this desire for riches becomes like an acid inside of us. It eats away at us with jealousy, bitterness and striving, until we are destroyed.

There are no "get-rich-quick" schemes. Wealth is not the product of schemes. Playing Lotto, pyramid selling, sweepstakes and the like will not yield wealth. As I have already mentioned, statistics show that those people who receive wealth this way normally lose it within the first five years.

I had an uncle who, every time he heard me preach, wrote down the reference numbers when I announced the sermon text. He felt that everything that came out of my mouth was anointed. However, when he got home, he didn't use the chapter and verse numbers to guide him in his Bible study. Instead, he used those numbers to play Lotto!

The story is amusing, but many of us are like this on the inside. We hold tightly to some irrational dream and scheme that we believe will yield wealth quickly. It is our fantasy and will never be realized, because wealth is built through wisdom, discipline and planning.

God's Financial Requirements

What does God require before He will release finances and other material blessings to us?

More than anything, God wants to be sure that we will not forget Him. It is all a matter of heart attitude. God wants to be central in our lives. He wants to be acknowledged as our source. Those of us who are parents have experienced this. When we buy gifts for our children, all we are looking for is a *grateful* heart.

David knew this principle. The entire book of Psalms is permeated with thanks to and acknowledgment of God.

> **Enter his gates with thanksgiving, and his courts with praise! Give thanks to him, bless his name!**
> **Psalm 100:4**

God's Tool

One word has probably become more meaningful to me this past year than any other word: *process*. In my pastoral capacity, I understand in a deeper way that we are all "in process." I have become very cautious about tampering with other peoples' lives in order to rescue them from difficult situations. God may be taking them through that very situation for a reason. If I short-circuit the process, God will have to find another way to mature the person in that particular area.

As humans, we tend to lack the broader view of process and see ourselves as locked into particular situations. As Christians, we need to come, not only to an understanding of process, but that the accumulation of wealth is also a part of the spiritual process God uses in our lives.

As part of the process, God may have us drive a beat-up car. That doesn't mean we're stuck with it for life or that God isn't going to prosper us. All it means is simply that at a certain point in the process, God is more interested in using a beat-up car to work out some area in our life than He is in getting us a new car.

Everyone, in some form or another, experiences this process. I do not know of one Christian, whether in ministry or in secular employment, who has not undergone some wilderness experience in the economic realm. God simply does not take us from spiritual newborn to mature Christian in one easy step. There are lessons to be learned along the way.

> **And you shall remember all the way which the Lord your God has led you these forty years in the wilderness.**
>
> **Deuteronomy 8:2**

For forty years, God had the Israelites in the wilderness. Forty years of process — forty years of humbling, molding and shaping their lives. God is no different with us.

We may be experiencing a lack of money, we may be living hand-to-mouth, paycheck to paycheck. God allows it. It is in these barren wilderness times in our lives that God burns into us the truth of remembering Him in all things. He is in the process of humbling us so we will know that our source is in Him. It's not something we can rebuke or pray the blood of Jesus against and cast out. It's the process of God working in our lives.

Fortunately, once we have learned our lessons, God doesn't leave us in the wilderness! The children of Israel went on to possess the land God had promised them and experienced all the prosperity and plenty that came with it! God will do the same for us.

If you are presently struggling through the wilderness, take heart. God is not leading you into poverty and financial hardship. He may be leading you *through it* as part of the process, but He will not leave you there.

Integrity

One of the most important qualities God wants to build

into our hearts is *integrity*. Integrity is a virtue with far higher value to God than our ability to make wealth. Integrity is putting our money where our mouth is. It is living out what we say we believe. Nowhere is this better demonstrated than in how we handle finances. When a situation touches our pocketbook, we really see what our priorities are. James tells us, **Faith apart from works is dead** (James 2:26). How do our financial "works" portray our faith?

God is interested in our financial situation, not primarily because He cares if we invest in CD's as opposed to bonds, but because money is a proving ground for our character. Money, more than anything I know, will tempt us into compromising our standards. God wants to see if He and our witness to others always take precedence over the drive to acquire money.

The last two years have been a period where God has directed me to invest more than ever before. It has also been a season where He has lavished financial blessings upon me. It has taken as much prayer to know what to do with the abundance He has provided as it did to pray for it when I had very little.

Wealth comes by grace. It takes the grace of God to maintain it, and it takes the grace of God to give it away. Many people are destroyed by wealth because they have not sought the grace to administer it in a godly way.

God Chooses the People He Wants to Bless

I believe God chooses the men and women He wants to bless. He chooses people who, in humility, have proven they can handle money and utilize it well to care for their family and for their own needs. They have also proven that should He require their money, they are willing to release it to the Kingdom of God as good stewards over that which He has given them.

God is the One Who chooses to give to us, and He is the One Who chooses to take away from us. In choosing, He assesses the integrity of our heart before Him.

I thank God that in His wisdom, He has chosen to take things from me. We are often blinded to the state of our own heart, and at times, God has used money to show me the state of my heart so I could deal with the issues.

Putting in the Effort

Charles J. Givens in his book, *Wealth Without Risk*, says financial success "requires first expending ten units of effort to produce one unit of results. Your momentum will then produce ten units of results with each unit of effort."[9]

As we think about this, we know it is true. If you are trying to become physically fit, the temptation to stay in bed the extra half hour in the morning is much stronger in the first week than it is once you have developed the habit of getting up and exercising.

When starting a manufacturing business, getting the first product ready to ship takes months of planning and a lot of finances. In comparison, shipping an order of the same product a year later takes minimal resources and time.

Don't be discouraged if your initial efforts yield small results in comparison to what you would like them to be. Tangible results take time to gather momentum.

> **And though your beginning was small, your latter days will be very great.**
>
> **Job 8:7**

In Closing

Many ideas have been presented in this book, some theological and some intensely practical. It would be unrealistic to think they could all be implemented at one time. Some of you have years of bad habits and misconceptions about God to undo.

Where do you begin? If you are married, you begin first by involving your partner in the process. Then you set a

---

[9]Givens, *Op. Cit.*, p. 23.

course and develop a strategy of accomplishing small attainable goals along the way to your ultimate goal of honoring God in your finances, and partnering with Him in building your wealth.

Don't let your present financial circumstances limit your thinking. Your present circumstances are not necessarily going to continue indefinitely. If you are in a financial wilderness, don't give up. There is a way through it. The wilderness is a place of training, not a permanent dwelling place. The children of Israel never looked upon their wilderness experience as permanent.

God orders our steps. If you follow His guidance and principles for handling money, you will experience better financial circumstances in the next one to five years.

> For I know the plans I have for you, says the Lord, plans for welfare and not for evil, to give you a future and a hope.
>
> Then you will call upon me and come and pray to me, and I will hear you.
>
> You will seek me and find me; when you seek me with all your heart,
>
> I will be found by you, says the Lord, and I will restore your fortunes....
>
> **Jeremiah 29:11-14**

About the Author

The ministry of Luther Blackwell is known literally around the world. Pastor Blackwell has traveled extensively as a lecturer, teacher and guest speaker for many groups, banquets, seminars and spiritual life events. He has been featured in some of the most prestigious and life-changing conferences in our nation and has graced pulpits of similar magnitude.

Pastor Blackwell presently serves as vice-president of the International Congress of Local Churches, which hosts a conference that ministers to 1,500 to 2,000 pastors worldwide. His music is heard through his nationally-acclaimed recording company, *Amplified Productions*, which specializes in providing sound tracks for congregational worship across the land. It is one of the first of its kind in the country.

In recent years, Pastor Blackwell has become known for his seminars on money and the black man. His two powerful tape series, **POWER TO GET WEALTH** and **BLACK HISTORY FROM GOD'S PERSPECTIVE,** are extremely popular, adding wealth and self-worth to its listeners. **BLACK HISTORY FROM GOD'S PERSPECTIVE** is presently being reviewed by leading Christian publishers for future release. His book, **FILLED TO PRAISE HIM,** has given valuable insight into understanding the dynamics of worship and praise.

Luther Blackwell is the pastor of two dynamic churches in Northeastern Ohio — New Life Fellowship, Cortland, and Mega Church, Cleveland. These churches are leaders in the area of multi-racial congregations, as they demonstrate the ability of God to bring His people together, though they are of different races and cultures.

Pastor Blackwell also serves as the overseer to churches on the Eastern seaboard. He is a pastor's pastor. His gifting extends to his television audience as he serves as one of the most popular hosts of ''Praise the Lord,'' a program viewed by hundreds of thousands on a local Trinity Broadcasting Network television station affiliate.

Pastor Blackwell, along with his wife, Lois, reside with their four beautiful children — Stacy Michelle, Alana Denise, Lucien Christopher and Meaghan Christina, in Cortland, Ohio.

Black History From God's Perspective

In this provocative tape series, Luther Blackwell unfolds the history of the Black race from it's Biblical origin. Throughout the series Pastor Blackwell emphasizes that: "These messages are not intended to glorify flesh". They are, however, to dissolve myths and bondages aquainted with Black history. Not only is this series a blessing to the Black race, but it will encourage all mankind to appreciate the uniqueness and values of the Black culture. A printed outline is included along with eight tapes for study purposes. $65.00 each. Tapes include:

*Who Am I?

*Importance of Genealogy

*From Whence Cometh the Black Man?

*Where Did They (Blacks) Go?

*Blacks (Probabilities) in Scripture

*Cursed Be Canaan

*Identifying the Black Man's God

*God, The Creator of Us All

Send to: Luther Blackwell Ministries
P.O. Box 174
Cortland, Ohio 44410-0174
(216) 638-7100
Please Include $3.00 Per Set For
Shipping and Handling Charges.

Please Allow Two Weeks Delivery

Dear Reader:

This series on Black History originated in my spirit as God spoke to me in January '91, and said, 'Pay attention to Black History Month.' This was a very unusual command to my heart, with me floundering as to how to properly execute that which I felt He had spoken so succinctly. Admittedly, Black History Month as well as the study of the Black man were topics to which I had previously given little attention. However, as I opened my heart thereto, God began fitting the pieces together in a rather extraordinary way. Thus, 'Black History From God's Perspective', was birthed.

May you, as you read this, understand more than anything what I am about to present. This series is only designed to give Blacks a working knowledge of their wonderfully rich Biblical heritage. May it also serve to inform non-Blacks of facts (scriptural) that have not heretofore been so readily espoused, giving a deep appreciation for their Black brethren.

In no way is it the intent of this author to exalt the superiority of any race, nor the inferiority of another, but only to exalt the Christ, Who is the 'Father' of all mankind, and to give Him all the glory respectfully due Him.

May you be found, at the conclusion of your study of this series on Black History, declaring the awesomeness of our God and affirming His fatherhood to all people.

Keeping Hope Alive,

Luther Blackwell

Please send me_____(number) of the "Black History..." series at $65.00 ea.

Please send me_____(number) of the "Power To Get Wealth" series at $75.00 ea.

Please send me_____(number) of the "Power To Get Wealth" series w/ book at $95.00 ea.

Enclosed is my check or money order for a sum of $_____ made payable to Luther Blackwell Ministries.

Here is my name and address. I am mailing in my order right away.

Name _____

Address _____

City_____ State_____ Zip_____

Additional outlines are available for group study. For more information phone: (216) 638-7100

WORSHIP By
AMPLIFIED
PRODUCTIONS

Amplified Productions is committed to the worship experience and to aid the local church to better glorify God through quality music. Our worship sound tracks provide the local church with quality music performance during its intimate time of worship; thus making this important time an experience that possibly would not otherwise be afforded the worshippers.

It is not at all the intention of Amplified Productions to replace the local church music ministry staff, but rather simply to enhance it with musicians, via worship sound tracks, who themselves understand worship and are indeed worshippers. Where there is total lack, the void will be filled.

Each Amplified Worship Sound Track is professionally recorded and produced on the highest quality stereo cassette. Our selections range from the latest popular choruses to the old-time favorites of traditional hymns. Choose from our selecton of pre-recorded songs or check out our custom made sound tracks exclusively designed for your congregation.

Library of Sounds
P.O. Box 174
Cortland, Ohio 44410-0174
(216) 638-5116

Amplified Productions is committed to the worship experience as well as to aiding the local church to better glorify God through quality music. Our worship sound tracks provide the local church with quality music performance during its intimate time of worship, thus making this important time an experience that possibly would not otherwise be afforded the worshippers.

LIST OF SOUND TRACKS

Amplified now features the Automatic Mailing Program
(one worship sound track per month)

HYMNS

*SPECIALTY

**WORSHIP BY AMPLIFIED

WIST-1
I'm Yours. The Center Of My Joy. I'm Looking For A
Greater Move Of God. God Has Not Given Us The Spirit
Of Fear. Anointing Fall On Me. See His Glory.

WIST-2
Ain't No Rock. Jesus Set Me Absolutely Free. Let Go. Let
God. O'Magnify The Lord. Shine Down. How Great Thou
Art.

**AMPLIFIED '90
VOL I
WIST-3

Come And Worship. He Who Began A Good Work In You.
I Have Been Washed. Oh How He Loves You and Me. I've
Got A Feeling. God Is Up To Something Good, Wonderful
Peace.

**AMPLIFIED '90
VOL II
WIST-4

Celebrate Jesus. Spirit Of Elijah. Shepherd Of My Soul.
Revelation 19. Great Is The Lord. God Has Not Given Us
The Spirit Of Fear. God Is Up To Something Good (vocal).
Turn Your Eyes Upon Jesus.

**HYMNS BY AMPLIFIED
WHIT-1

Standing On The Promises. What A Friend We Have In
Jesus. Blessed Assurance. Amazing Grace (Praise God).
Leaning On The Everlasting Arms. Jesus Loves Me. This
I Know. The Solid Rock. How Great Thou Art.

**WHATEVER YOU DESIRE
Featuring Valeria Long
WVST-1

Whatever You Desire. I Will Bless The Lord. Sons And
Daughters. I Miss My Time With You.

WVST-2

Jesus Is Alive. I Want To Be More Like You. Move Again,
Rain On Our Fields.

SOUND TRACKS

*"You don't need music to
worship...but it helps."*

"Committed to the worship experience."
All Sound Tracks — $8.95
*Specialty — $19.95
**Packaged Tapes — $10.00

Entire Library Of Sounds — $600.00
Plus Shipping and Handling

Order From List On Opposite Side
Add $1.50 For Shipping
For Every Six Tapes

Please Allow Two Weeks For Delivery

Send to: Amplified Productions
P.O. Box 174/Cortland, Ohio 44410-0174
Office phone number is (216) 638-5118

Please send me (total no. of tapes)_____ at $8.95 each.

Please send me (total no. of tapes)_____ at $10.00 each.

Please send me (total no. of tapes)_____ at $19.95 each.

Please send me the entire Library at $600.00 _____.

Ohio Residents Add 5% Sales Tax

Enclosed is my check or money order for the sum of $_____ made payable
to Amplified Productions.

Here is my name and address. I am mailing in my order right away.

Name _____

Address _____

City_____ State_____ Zip_____